THE JANUS FACTOR

Since 1996, Bloomberg Press has published books for financial professionals on investing, economics, and policy affecting investors. Titles are written by leading practitioners and authorities, and have been translated into more than 20 languages.

The Bloomberg Financial Series provides both core reference knowledge and actionable information for financial professionals. The books are written by experts familiar with the work flows, challenges, and demands of investment professionals who trade the markets, manage money, and analyze investments in their capacity of growing and protecting wealth, hedging risk, and generating revenue.

For a list of available titles, visit our Web site at www.wiley.com/go/bloombergpress.

THE JANUS FACTOR

Trend Follower's Guide
to Market Dialectics

Gary Edwin Anderson

BLOOMBERG PRESS
An Imprint of
WILEY

For general information on our other products and services or for technical support, please contact
our Customer Care Department within the United States at (800) 762-2974, outside the United States
at (317) 572-3993 or fax (317) 572-4002.

Wiley also publishes its books in a variety of electronic formats. Some content that appears in print
may not be available in electronic books. For more information about Wiley products, visit our web site
at www.wiley.com.

Library of Congress Cataloging-in-Publication Data:

Anderson, Gary Edwin, 1942-
    The Janus factor : trend follower's guide to market dialectics / Gary Edwin Anderson.
       p. cm.
    Includes index.
    ISBN 978-1-118-08707-7 (cloth); ISBN 978-1-118-23600-0 (ebk);
    ISBN 978-1-118-26169-9 (ebk); ISBN 978-1-118-22348-2 (ebk)
       1. Speculation. 2. Investment analysis. 3. Investments. I. Title.
HG6015.A526 1012
332.64—dc23

                                                                          2012030690

For
Carol Anne

The Janus Factor

Ja'nus: Early Roman god of gates and portals, suggesting the two sides of a door. Represented by two opposing faces, Janus symbolizes the two-sided nature of things.

Contents

Introduction

In this Discourse I do not undertake to say all that is known, or may be said of it, but I undertake to acquaint the Reader with many things that are not usually known to every Angler; and I shall leave gleanings and observations enough to be made out of the experience of all that love and practise this recreation, to which I shall encourage them. For Angling may be said to be so like the Mathematicks, that it can never be fully learnt; at least not so fully, but that there will still be more new experiments left for the trial of other men that succeed us. But I think all that love this game may here learn something that may be worth their money, if they be not poor and needy men: and in case they be, I then wish them to forbear to buy it; for I write not to get money, but for pleasure, and this Discourse boasts of no more, for I hate to promise much, and deceive the Reader.
—Izaak Walton, *The Compleat Angler*, 1653

This book embraces both theory and craft. In the first five chapters, I present a systematic view of the market, not as a battle between buyers and sellers, or even between bulls and bears, but as a struggle for dominance by traders holding to radically opposed paradigms. A new measure of risk is offered, and on that theoretical foundation I build a method.

Craft confronts a real world of noisy data and thorny reality, so in the remaining six chapters I apply these methods to the historical record. In the final three I detail strategic indicators, which readers may use to guide day-to-day trading decisions.

Some of what I demonstrate is, so far as I know, taught nowhere else. The main ideas presented in this book are simple but crucial for anyone who wishes to trade successfully in all market environments.

Acknowledgments

Writing a book, I have come to learn, is a lonely pursuit, but a number of friends and colleagues cheered me along and some have contributed to the book's content and finish.

First among those is my wife, Carol Anne. Her trust and support made it impossible for me to disappoint her. My friend and former business partner, Jack Loe, not only encouraged me, but his practical insights are sprinkled throughout the book.

There are others I wish to thank as well. Toni Turner is a successful author of books on trading, and from the beginning her natural optimism repeatedly refreshed me and my determination. I wish to thank Dr. Timothy Masters for his edits of technical issues, which have spared me from numerous small embarrassments. Nelson Freeburg lent his keen eye and broad knowledge of quantitative systems. David Aronson has been a friend of the project.

Finally, I wish to acknowledge those whose words and work I have borrowed freely.

To steal ideas from one person is plagiarism. To steal from many is research.

—*Wilson Mizner,* 1938

CHAPTER 1

Foundations

Every autobiography is the fragment of a theory.
—Leigh Gilmore, *The Limits of Autobiography*[1]

The young meteorologist started his computer run and walked down the hall for a cup of coffee. When he returned, the direction of both his life and his science had radically shifted. Ed Lorenz was experimenting with models of the weather on an early desk-sized computer. His research project called for him to input variables for atmospheric conditions and then let the computer grind out future weather patterns according to well-established algorithms based on meteorological laws. On this occasion, he decided to repeat an earlier computation in order to examine longer-term output in more detail. Normally, the computer ran these calculations from beginning to end in one take, but to save time Lorenz decided to start nearer to the point of his interest rather than to redo the entire run. As initial conditions he typed in a line of numbers printed midway during an earlier computation, started the program, and left the room. His coffee break lasted about an hour.

On his return, he expected to find an identical copy of his previous weather simulation, but the numbers now churning from the computer did not match the earlier version. At first he suspected a weak vacuum tube, but on closer inspection of the output he noticed that while values repeated previous results early on, the new numbers being printed out gradually diverged from the old. The difference between the two series doubled periodically until finally, near the end of the run, results differed wildly.

> This was enough to tell me what had happened: the numbers that I had typed in were not the exact original numbers, but were the rounded-off values that had appeared in the original printout. The initial round-off errors were the culprits; they were steadily amplifying until they dominated the solution. In today's terminology, there was chaos.[2]

The computer employed six decimal places during computation but printed results to only three. The data Lorenz entered from the earlier printout was off by three decimal places, a very small amount but enough to generate a very large difference in results. Lorenz dubbed this phenomenon the "butterfly effect"[3] to make his point that small changes in initial conditions, even the flapping of a butterfly's wings, could theoretically produce large-scale changes in the weather. "It soon struck me," Lorenz wrote, "that if the real atmosphere behaved like the simple model, long-range forecasting would be impossible."[4] This insight, born of Lorenz's error, ultimately forced analysts to rethink the dynamics of deterministic systems and, in the process, led to a novel line of inquiry now referred to as chaos theory.

This was Lorenz's first inkling that small differences early on could radically alter outcomes. His own career would become a prime example. Had Lorenz followed protocol and begun the program at the beginning rather than in the middle, his role in a new branch of mathematics might have been delayed or perhaps not materialized. But that's life. We all know how small events can lead to important changes. Miss your bus by five minutes and miss the commuter train by an hour. Miss the train, and meet your future wife. Or make the bus and meet your future wife. Sleep in, arrive too late for the interview, and your career path changes. In science, as in life, it often comes down to the smallest details of biography.

Serendipity

My father sat in his recliner, reading the evening paper, dropping pages to the floor as he read them. Sprawled on the carpet—I might have been watching

Flash Gordon or Gene Autry on our black and white Hoffman TV—I began carelessly to read the financial section. Scanning up and down the columns of data, I spotted a stock selling for around $3, a price I could relate to. The company mined silver, and I imagined miners with picks and shovels filling car after car with valuable rocks, like the miners I had seen in movies.

I followed the stock for a few days before I noticed the volume increase sharply, though the price rose only modestly. The same thing happened the next day. For some reason, I became convinced that the stock would triple, and I announced that prediction to my dad. Why a triple? I'm not sure what reasoning, if any, led to that conclusion. In the absence of any method, perhaps I found the symmetry of three times $3 appealing.

Amazingly, the stock moved to $9 within a few days. Of course, it was just a fluke, an odd coincidence with no wider meaning. On the other hand, had I guessed wrong that day, would I be telling this story? A lucky guess on one long-ago summer evening sparked a lifelong interest in the market and, more specifically, in the analysis of price-volume.

What leads us to the methods we eventually adopt for ourselves? What makes us see things the way we do? The answers, it seems to me, are mostly anecdotal. But if an analytical approach is rooted in some accident of biography, how can we legitimize our choice of method? Shouldn't method be supported by rigorous appeal to objective reality?

I do not know how it is with you, but for myself I generally give up at the outset. The simplest problems which come up from day to day seem to me quite unanswerable as soon as I try to get below the surface.

—*Justice Learned Hand*[5]

Most of us, if asked, would express confidence in an objective reality that lies just below the surface, beyond appearances. Albert Einstein shared that belief, but late in his career he confronted two irreconcilable versions of physical reality. His own theory of relativity assumes continuous space and time, whereas quantum theory introduces the idea that space and time are not continuous at all scales but are finally reducible to indivisible lumps, or quanta. Einstein believed that because each theory offered only a partial account, each was inadequate, and that a deeper mining of reality would ultimately provide a comprehensive narrative superseding both.

However, Einstein was also keenly aware of the limits to our knowledge. He began one of his essays with this sentence:

> Belief in an external world independent of the percipient subject is the foundation of all science.[6]

Einstein could have advanced a stronger, unqualified statement:

> An external world independent of the percipient subject is the foundation of all science.

But he did not. Perhaps he was just being careful, and chose to avoid a murky issue better left to metaphysics. In any case, clearly he, along with Learned Hand, found the notion of objective reality problematic. Nevertheless, each likely accepted as an article of faith, as most of us do, the existence of an "external world independent of the percipient subject" that warrants experience and, at bottom, makes sense.

In the work of Isaac Newton, faith in deterministic rationality reached its zenith. Since laws of motion regulate the position and velocity of a body, if the initial states of both are known, then the trajectory of the body is uniquely determined. The French mathematician Pierre-Simon Laplace penned this classic statement of the determinist creed one century after the success of Newton's *Principia*:

> An intellect which at a certain moment would know all forces that set nature in motion, and all positions of all items of which nature is composed, if this intellect were also vast enough to submit these data to analysis, it would embrace in a single formula the movements of the greatest bodies of the universe and those of the tiniest atom; for such an intellect nothing would be uncertain and the future just like the past would be present before its eyes.[7]

If, like Laplace's demon,[8] we knew "all forces that set nature in motion, and all positions of all items of which nature is composed," we could confidently predict tomorrow's weather, the next winner of the Kentucky Derby, or the path of the market. The problem, of course, is that we are not all-knowing. Our vision is narrow, as if we were peering through a tube. Rather than seeing the world as a coherent whole, what we know, or think we know, consists of a patchwork of ideas, stories, traditions, theories, lists, manuals, folklore, habits, standards, rules of thumb, and procedures.

Because we build explanatory systems out of materials within the range of our own experience, our attempt to make sense of things is mostly serendipitous and necessarily autobiographical. In the end, a particular way of seeing the world, informed by culture and personal history, emerges. What is revealed may not ascend to truth, but—if we are lucky—to a more or less useful way forward.

The Data Set

The success of any investigation depends on the judicious selection of what is to be observed.

—*James C. Maxwell*[9]

Traders are drawn to all sorts of data, including price-volume, fundamentals, market cycles, and astrology. The amount and varieties of available data challenge our limited ability to process information, so choices must be made. Perhaps out of mere accident, for me the choice of price-volume as the object of research came easily. But now that my choice has been made, or made for me, I will venture a soft defense of my preference.

Skeptics hold that operations based only on observed price changes cannot succeed. Markets are moved by news, they argue, and since, by definition, news cannot be predicted (or it would not be news), price movement cannot be anticipated. It is a short step to conclude that price data are not linked and that price series follow a random walk.

Skeptics fail to take into account that price activity is also news. Traders respond to news of price change just as they respond to other sorts of news. By their collective response, traders forge links between past price data and current price movement. Price data are linked because traders link them.

Of all alternatives, the set of business and economic data is the most broadly accepted, in part because fundamentals sport a data set larger and more open than price-volume. For some, the richness of fundamental data is an advantage, but for me the openness, the inexhaustibility, of fundamental news is a liability. Broadening analysis to include economic data does not make things easier, since economic data is harder to come by and unlimited. How much information is enough? An old joke makes the point: A little girl came home from school and exclaimed, "Today we learned to spell banana, but we didn't learn when to stop!"

Any system is defined by the boundary between itself and its environment, and price data comprise a system that is both finite and well defined. Publication is more or less immediate. Data is cheap and available to all simultaneously. The problem is not the availability of data, or that there is too much or too little data. The problem, or rather the potential solution, lies in properly decoding the data. That is what I found interesting from the start and what has driven my investigations in the years since.

Reasons and Causes

There is always a reason for a stock acting the way it does. But also remember that chances are you will not become acquainted with that reason until some time in the future, when it is too late to act on it profitably.

—Jesse Livermore[10]

The link between fundamentals and price is elastic. At times strong earnings buoy the price of a security, while at other times positive earnings prompt traders to sell. Will a crisis increase the value of the dollar or send it lower? The linkage between change in the world-at-large and change in the market is often ambiguous and sometimes just mysterious. In most cases, human beings are clever enough to devise plausible stories to account for the market's response to events, but too often only with the aid of hindsight.

There is a constant shift in the fundamental rationale used to support decisions to buy and sell. During the 1960s, synergy became a popular concept. The stocks of companies successful at acquiring other companies were bid up aggressively on the theory that, in the stock market at least, $2 + 2 = 5$. However, during the 1970s, after a series of bear markets had chastened investors, conservative analysis of book value and dividend history, not the synergy of the go-go years, provided a very different rationale for traders' decisions.

A dramatic change in the culture of investing took place in Japan during the 1960s. Japanese traders traditionally viewed equities as a form of high-risk bonds. Stocks were purchased based on the strength of dividends, and the growth of earnings was largely ignored. When American traders discovered the Japanese stock market, they found that price-to-earnings ratios for Japanese stocks were far lower than for comparable U.S. issues. To the Japanese, local equities were fairly priced, but for Americans, Japanese stocks were bargains. Americans began to buy Japanese issues massively, based on an investment rationale imported from America. Almost overnight, the culture of Japanese investing changed, and one of the great bull markets in history was launched.

There is no disputing the importance of traders' reasons for buying and selling. People routinely use reasons to support decisions of all sorts, and trading decisions are important enough to merit important reasons. However, as the above illustrations demonstrate, fundamental conventions supporting trading decisions can vary from period to period and from place to place.

We may draw a useful distinction between reasons and causes. Earnings do not cause prices to move, neither do research reports, news bulletins, dividends, stock splits, the economy, peace, nor war. These factors may be reasons motivating traders to buy and sell, but the direct cause of securities' price movement is the buying and selling activity of traders.[11] This book focuses on causes, not reasons—on what traders do, not why. Of course, we will tell stories, too, but our stories do not shed much, if any, light on traders' reasons. Instead, they offer a context for making sense of traders' actions.

Befuddled

I found everything perfectly clear, and I really understood absolutely nothing. To understand is to change, to go beyond oneself.

—*Jean-Paul Sartre*[12]

I arrived a few minutes late. The session was already underway, so I took the last available chair in the back row. On a screen behind the broker were patterns traced by stock prices. He gave them names and explained what each portends. Near the end of the session, an older gentleman in the chair next to mine leaned over and whispered, "If you want to understand how the market really works, call this number." He handed me a scrap of paper.

How odd it seems to me now, more than 40 years later, that had I arrived a few minutes earlier I might have missed a chance encounter and small gesture that again altered the course of my life. On the scrap he had written the number for Wyckoff Associates in Park Ridge, Illinois.

At $22 per month, the Wyckoff correspondence course was expensive for a graduate student, but with the gracious consent of my wife, who at the time supported us both, I enrolled. Over the next two years I drew by hand, and puzzled over, hundreds of charts, and I listened to dozens of taped lessons. It was not long before my interest in studying the market overtook my interest in reading dead philosophers.

Richard Wyckoff founded the *Magazine of Wall Street* in 1907, and over the decades, as trader, teacher, and financial writer, he developed a deep understanding of the moment-to-moment struggle waged between buyers and sellers. Perhaps the most important thing I learned from him was that the proper object of study is not something we call "the market" but rather the collective intent of investors and traders, who reinvent the market daily. If that is so, then patterns in the data cannot be enough since they do not account for what is distinctively human behind the tape.

Wyckoff wrote his course in the 1930s, and its content was no doubt shaped by his experience of the 1929 crash and the post-crash period. The market of the early 1930s was lively in both directions, and anyone who survived and succeeded during those turbulent times necessarily developed a keen appreciation for market risk. For that reason, perhaps, he stressed methods that were both risk averse and contrarian.

Contrarian traders focus not on trends, but on changes in the trends of stocks and of the overall market. Contrarians tend to buy sold-out issues, usually before upward trends are broadly recognized. On the other hand, contrarian traders are ever alert for signs that a rising market should be sold.

My introduction to live trading began during the go-go years of the 1960s. The market at the time was trending powerfully, and the leading issues were, nearly without exception, trading well above their lows and showed no signs of tiring as day after day, week after week, they climbed to new highs.

The dominant feature of the market during those years was its continuing trend. However, whatever edge I had then depended on my ability to spot changes in the trend. I was soon completely befuddled. Stocks that lagged continued to languish, while strongly trending stocks rolled right through levels of intense selling. A contrarian in a trending market, I was like a plumber who had been called out to repair the electrical wiring. The skills I had worked so hard to develop seemed irrelevant. I still had much to learn, and the market itself became my teacher.

FIGURE 1.1 Dow Jones Industrial Average—January 1963 through mid-February 1966

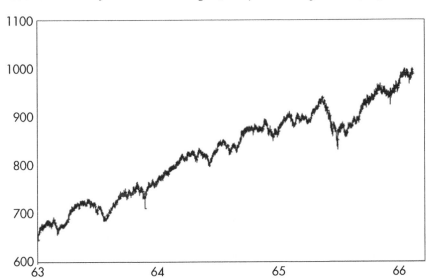

Which Way Is Up?

Never trade in a market which does not show a definite trend. You are just
guessing.

—*Orline D. Foster*[13]

Eddie Toppel speaks with a wry, pixie glint in his eyes. Much more is
meant, one suspects, than is said. Addressing a conference of technical traders
some years ago, Eddie, then a 22-year veteran of Chicago's futures and
options pits, pointed his finger toward the ceiling without preamble. "What
direction is this?" he asked. A wary silence fell over the gathered technicians,
as if he had asked a trick question. "Up!" someone ventured. "Right!" Eddie
responded. "This is easy!" He pointed his finger down. "And which way is
this?" Together the audience cried, "Down!"

"You learn quickly!" It was clear that Eddie was having fun. "It's simple.
When they are going up, buy 'em, and when they are going down, sell 'em.
The secret of success is knowing which way is up."

There are some who, having perceived clearly the failure of price predictions, conclude that markets are random and unknowable. Against those claims, I maintain that there is something we can know: the presence or absence of a trend. Without the occasional emergence of trends, market price series would be truly random and radical cynicism justified. Fortunately, trends happen. As Tom Basso points out:

> If there were no trends, you could expect a fairly random distribution of price changes. Yet if you look at the distribution of price changes over time in almost any market, you'll see a very long tail in the direction of large price changes. This is because there are abnormally large price changes that you'd never expect to see by chance over a given period of time.[14]

It is the trend, and only the trend, that offers profit. Overbought/oversold indicators, trading setups, the patterns we read into charts might help clarify, or not, might embolden the trader to take a position, or not. But there is no device or trading trick that makes the trader money. Only the trend can do that.

Traders face a practical problem, however. Price moves incessantly, at times arcing in sustained trends while at other times twisting back upon itself. At what point, and how, is the trader to determine that a nascent price trend is likely to continue? When Jack D. Schwager, the author of *Market Wizards*, interviewed trend trader Richard Dennis, he asked, "Is there something special that you look for to define a trend?" Dennis's answer was to the point: "No."[15] In the absence of independent evidence of a trend, Dennis's response makes sense. The notion of a self-warranting trend is tautological and empty. If there is some mark or feature that verifies trends, it cannot be merely that trends persist, since that is the question at issue.

Trend followers cited in Schwager's book look for independent evidence to help verify trends, and the nature of that evidence can shift based on general conditions. As Bruce Kovner observes in *Market Wizards*, "the rules of the trading and investment game keep changing."[16]

So the question remains. Is there a property of trends, or evidence of some dynamic, that might help traders identify reliable trends early on, even before a trade is taken? The search for this missing observable led to insights that form the foundation for methods presented in this book.

Notes

1. Leigh Gilmore, *The Limits of Autobiography* (Ithaca, NY: Cornell University, 2001).
2. Edward N. Lorenz, *The Essence of Chaos* (Seattle: University of Washington Press, 1993).
3. Edward N. Lorenz, "Predictability: Does the Flap of a Butterfly's Wings in Brazil Set Off a Tornado in Texas?" (address at the American Association for the Advancement of Science, Boston, MA, December 29, 1972).
4. Ibid.
5. Learned Hand, "Democracy: Its Presumptions and Realities," in *The Spirit of Liberty: Papers and Addresses of Learned Hand*, collected by Irving Dillard, 3rd ed. (New York: Alfred A. Knopf, 1960), 92–93.
6. Albert Einstein, "Clerk Maxwell's Influence on the Evolution of the Idea of Physical Reality" (1931), in *The World As I See It* (London: John Lane the Bodely Head, 1935).
7. Pierre-Simon, Marquis de Laplace, *Essai philosophique sur les probabilités* (Paris: Courcier, 1814).
8. In commentaries on Laplace's work, *intellect* is often referred to as Laplace's *demon*.
9. James C. Maxwell, quoted in Gerard M. Weinberg, *An Introduction to General Systems Thinking* (New York: John Wiley & Sons, 1975).
10. Jesse Livermore, *How to Trade in Stocks* (New York: Duell, Sloan and Pearce, 1940).
11. Whether a short-term trader or long-term investor, any person or institution dealing in either long or short equities is speculating. In this book I use the term *trader* to mean anyone who buys or sells shares.
12. Jean-Paul Sartre, *Search for a Method* (New York: Vintage Books, 1960).
13. Orline D. Foster, *Ticker Technique* (New York: Investors' Press, 1965).
14. Tom Basso, in Van K. Tharp, *Trade Your Way to Financial Freedom* (New York: McGraw-Hill, 1999).
15. Jack D. Schwager, *Market Wizards: Interviews with Top Traders* (New York: New York Institute of Finance, 1989).
16. Ibid.

CHAPTER 2

The Assignment

I must create a system or be enslaved by another man's.
— William Blake, "Jerusalem"

Nearly two decades ago, our fledgling firm took on a new client, a professional corporation with a retirement plan. The principals asked us to rate money managers bidding to run the plan's assets. Rating money managers was not our normal business, but we could not afford to turn away a new client. Over the next few weeks, we prepared a tutorial for trustees on the fundamentals of modern portfolio theory (MPT). Since MPT equates risk with standard deviation, or volatility, the way to reduce risk, according to the theory, is to reduce portfolio volatility. That bit of magic is accomplished by including investments that zig as other portfolio investments zag. The idea is that opposing swings in investments serve to cancel each other out, thus smoothing volatility and reducing risk.

We made our presentation to board members. At the end of the session, we invited questions. There were none. We assumed that we had anticipated and answered all of their concerns satisfactorily. Later, we found out differently.

Our analysis perplexed them. In particular, our use of standard deviation to measure risk left them profoundly uneasy. They understood the sense in which volatility is risky, but as a definition, *volatility* did not cover what they understood by *risk*.

Could we come up with a more intuitive measure of risk? To be relevant, a workable definition should take into account the practical concerns of investors, and to communicate effectively our language would have to remain true to ordinary meanings. I wanted something my mother would understand.

A method that everyone understands has to be based on what everyone already knows, so we asked clients and associates an elementary question. Why do investors hire portfolio managers? The answers coming back were consistent and not very surprising: Investors hire managers (1) to create gains, and (2) to protect capital against loss.

Measuring Risk: Offense and Defense

Markets are risky. And risk, everyone knows, involves loss, or the possibility of loss. The connection we all make between risk and loss is intuitive and powerful. Because the probability of equity loss increases as markets fall, we reasoned that a manager's ability to defend capital against loss is most critically tested during periods of market decline.

But rising markets are risky, too. Regardless how well managers defend against loss during falling markets, if they are unable to earn satisfactory returns, they subject clients to another risk, lost opportunity. Since opportunity-risk is always highest as the broad market advances, that form of risk is best measured when the market is rising.

Managers' returns are reported quarterly, so our first task was to determine how many quarters should be included in our performance review. After consulting clients, we settled on five years, or 20 quarters. Having identified two sorts of risks, we devised a way to measure each against a benchmark. *Merriam-Webster's Collegiate Dictionary* defines a benchmark as "something that serves as a standard by which others may be referenced or judged." Since we were measuring managers against their peers, to construct our benchmark we summed the median quarterly performance of all managers under analysis.[1]

We use two sets of benchmark returns, one to measure offensive performance and the other to measure defensive performance. Successive 20-quarter periods are analyzed. Offensive returns include only those greater than or equal to the benchmark's median return over 20 quarters, while a second set of defensive returns includes the balance of the benchmark's quarterly returns, those less than the median.

In Table 2.1, hypothetical quarterly returns for the benchmark are shown in column A. The median return of those 20 quarterly returns is 1.92.

TABLE 2.1 Benchmark, Offensive, and Defensive Returns

	A	B	C
	Benchmark Returns	Offensive Returns	Defensive Returns
1	2.49	2.49	
2	−4.23		−4.23
3	3.63	3.63	
4	1.87		1.87
5	−1.01		−1.01
6	5.76	5.76	
7	3.41	3.41	
8	−2.16		−2.16
9	−1.49		−1.49
10	−0.85		−0.85
11	5.23	5.23	
12	0.03		0.03
13	3.94	3.94	
14	4.19	4.19	
15	−2.61		−2.61
16	−0.05		−0.05
17	0.95		0.95
18	3.85	3.85	
19	2.73	2.73	
20	1.97	1.97	

In column B, returns greater than or equal to 1.92 are logged, and the balance of the returns, those less than the benchmark, are shown in column C.

In Table 2.2, three more columns are added. Column D shows one hypothetical manager's quarterly returns over five years. In columns E and F, the manager's quarterly returns are sorted in accordance with the sorting of benchmark returns in columns B and C. That is, if the benchmark's quarterly return falls under "Offensive," then the manager's return is also registered under "Offensive"; otherwise the return is counted as "Defensive."

TABLE 2.2 Manager's Offense and Defense

	A	B	C	D	E	F
	Benchmark Returns	Benchmark Offensive Returns	Benchmark Defensive Returns	Manager's Returns	Manager's Offensive Returns	Manager's Defensive Returns
1	2.49	2.49		3.67	3.67	
2	−4.23		−4.23	−1.34		−1.34
3	3.63	3.63		5.54	5.54	
4	1.87		1.87	0.89		0.89
5	−1.01		−1.01	−2.06		−2.06
6	5.76	5.76		6.76	6.76	
7	3.41	3.41		3.70	3.70	
8	−2.16		−2.16	−3.54		−3.54
9	−1.49		−1.49	−1.07		−1.07
10	−0.85		−0.85	0.96		0.96
11	5.23	5.23		3.62	3.62	
12	0.03		0.03	2.16		2.16
13	3.94	3.94		2.69	2.69	
14	4.19	4.19		6.71	6.71	
15	−2.61		−2.61	−3.84		−3.84
16	−0.05		−0.05	0.19		0.19
17	0.95		0.95	−0.43		−0.43
18	3.85	3.85		2.75	2.75	
19	2.73	2.73		5.37	5.37	
20	1.97	1.97		0.83	0.83	

The sum of the manager's quarterly offensive returns over the five years is 41.64. That amount is divided by 37.20, the sum of the benchmark's offensive returns (column B) for same quarters. A result of 1.12 is multiplied by 100 to arrive at the manager's offensive score of 112. A score higher than 100 indicates that the manager's offensive returns were better than the benchmark's over the five-year period.

A similar computation determines the manager's defensive score. The sum of the manager's defensive returns, −8.08, is divided by −9.55, the sum of the benchmark's defensive returns. The manager's defensive score is −8.08/ −9.55, or .85. Again, that amount is multiplied by 100. A score below 100 indicates better-than-benchmark defense. With a defensive score of 85, our manager lost less than his peers during periods of higher-than-median return.

We reviewed hundreds of performance records. Some managers, we discovered, won by executing a good offense, and others by executing an exceptional defense. The best managers we surveyed combined superior offense with superior defense.

Picturing Offense and Defense

In Figure 2.1, the vertical axis displays offensive performance. A score above 100 indicates that the target manager's offensive return exceeds the benchmark's over the same quarters. A weak offense underperforms the benchmark and earns a score below 100.

Defensive performance is shown along the horizontal axis (see Figure 2.2). Strong defense scores less than 100, indicating that defensive losses, if any, are less than the benchmark's. On the other hand, weak defense

FIGURE 2.1 Picturing Offense

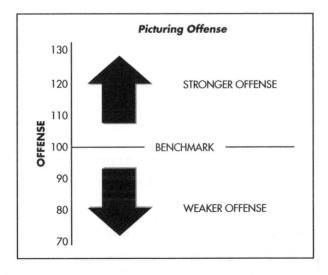

FIGURE 2.2   Picturing Defense

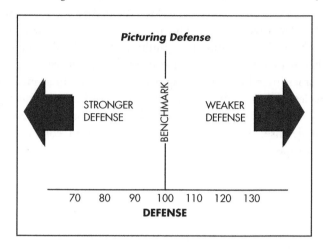

FIGURE 2.3   Offense and Defense Performance

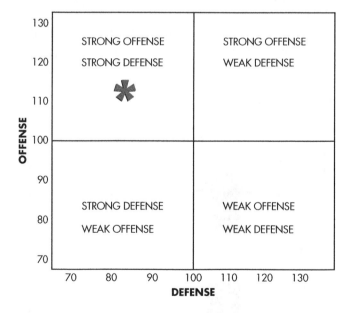

produces results that are worse than the benchmark's over those same periods and is indicated by a defensive score higher than 100.

Figure 2.3 combines offensive and defensive performance into one graphic display. Strong performance along both axes lands a manager in the northwest (NW) quadrant, while weak performance on both counts puts the manager in the southeast (SE) quadrant. The other two quadrants locate managers with mixed results. With an offensive score of 112 and a defensive score of 85, our manager has outperformed the benchmark both offensively and defensively and earns a spot in the NW quadrant.

The Benchmark Equivalence Line (BEL)

Since the benchmark is equal to itself, its offensive and defensive scores are 1.00 and 1.00, or 100 and 100, respectively. Those scores put the benchmark at the intersection of the horizontal and vertical axes. Suppose, however, that we increase the volatility of the benchmark by multiplying benchmark returns by, say, 1.2. Column D in Table 2.3 shows increased returns for the new benchmark-as-target (BAT). To compute the offensive score, the BAT's offensive returns are summed and divided by the sum of the original benchmark's returns. The result is 1.2, or an offensive score of 120. Computing the BAT's defensive score yields the same result, 120.

There are infinite combinations of benchmark offense and defense that differ in volatility but are equivalent in relative performance. The offensive and defensive scores of these combinations range from exceedingly weak offense and very strong defense to the other extreme of excellent offense together with poor defense. Benchmark-equivalent combinations fall along a southwest–northeast diagonal that passes through the intersection of offensive and defensive benchmarks (100–100) and make up the benchmark equivalence line (BEL), shown in Figure 2.4 (page 21).

Offensive–defensive scores that place managers anywhere NW of the BEL demonstrate relative performance that is better than the benchmark at equivalent volatilities, while placement SW of the BEL indicates performance worse than the benchmark (see Figure 2.5 on page 21). The further a target is to the northeast (NE), the more volatile it is relative to the original benchmark. Targets to the SW of 100–100 are less volatile than the benchmark.

We may reduce the volatility of the benchmark until returns equal zero, or the performance of cash. At that point we have reached 0–0 on the benchmark (see Figure 2.6 on page 22). Benchmark returns to the SW of 0–0 correlate negatively to the original benchmark returns, and the further to the SW of 0–0, the greater are the volatilities of negatively correlated returns.

In Figure 2.6, D and E underperformed the benchmark and are located southeast (SE) of the BEL. E is SW of 100–100 and therefore less volatile than the benchmark. A, G, and B all performed relatively better than the benchmark

TABLE 2.3 Benchmark-as-Target (BAT) Returns

	A	B	C	D	E	F
	Benchmark Returns	Benchmark Offensive Returns	Benchmark Defensive Returns	Benchmark × 1.2 (BAT)	BAT Offense	BAT Defense
1	2.49	2.49		2.99	2.99	
2	−4.23		−4.23	−5.08		−5.08
3	3.63	3.63		4.36	4.36	
4	1.87		1.87	2.24		2.24
5	−1.01		−1.01	−1.21		−1.21
6	5.76	5.76		6.91	6.91	
7	3.41	3.41		4.09	4.09	
8	−2.16		−2.16	−2.59		−2.59
9	−1.49		−1.49	−1.79		−1.79
10	−0.85		−0.85	−1.02		−1.02
11	5.23	5.23		6.28	6.28	
12	0.03		0.03	0.04		0.04
13	3.94	3.94		4.73	4.73	
14	4.19	4.19		5.03	5.03	
15	−2.61		−2.61	−3.13		−3.13
16	−0.05		−0.05	−0.06		−0.06
17	0.95		0.95	1.14		1.14
18	3.85	3.85		4.62	4.62	
19	2.73	2.73		3.28	3.28	
20	1.97	1.97		2.36	2.36	

and are, therefore, to the NW of the BEL. B and C are more volatile than the benchmark. Since C and F are on the BEL, relative performance in each case is equal to the benchmark's. F matches the benchmark's performance through a combination of superior defense and inferior offense. F is, however, less volatile than the benchmark. H is negatively correlated to the benchmark and more volatile than cash (0–0).

FIGURE 2.4   The Benchmark Equivalence Line (BEL)

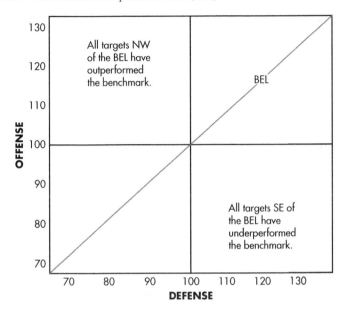

FIGURE 2.5   Volatility

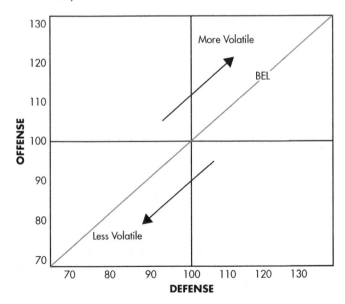

FIGURE 2.6 Sample Targets

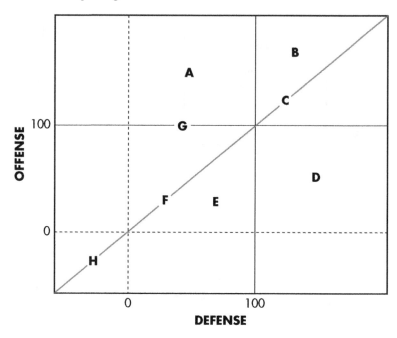

The Trend of Relative Performance

The trend of a manager's relative performance may be tracked against the background of our matrix by linking successive calculations of offensive–defensive performance. In Figure 2.7 the target manager's performance improves over time relative to that of peer performance, from a weak position offensively and defensively toward improvement both offensively and defensively.

In Figure 2.8, relative performance moves in the opposite direction, from strength to weakness. The trend of performance declines over time, both offensively and defensively.

Then we made a conceptual leap. Why not employ our new techniques to reveal the offensive and defensive characteristics of individual stocks and industry groups? To test this new idea I selected stocks from the S&P 100 plus the NASDAQ 100, then, using a six-month look-back, I plotted the relative strength of the 200 stocks[2] against our offensive–defensive matrix. Figure 2.9 shows the matrix of stocks as of November 4, 1996.

FIGURE 2.7 Positive Trend of Relative Strength

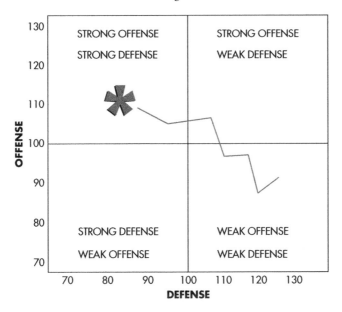

FIGURE 2.8 Negative Trend of Relative Performance

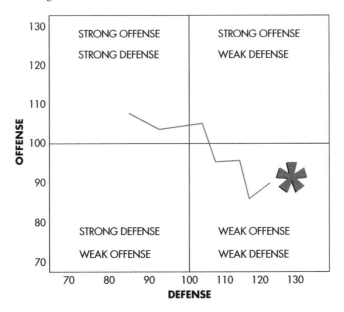

FIGURE 2.9   200-Stock Matrix—November 4, 1996

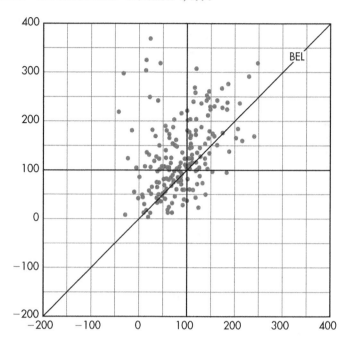

I plotted the matrix over succeeding periods. I could not have anticipated what I found. The cluster of stocks expanded and then contracted back toward the BEL, before expanding again. What accounts for this dynamic? And what are its practical implications, if any? Those questions are taken up in the Chapter 3.

Notes

1. **How to Build a Benchmark:** A benchmark can be a broad market index such as the S&P 500, a sector or group index, or an average made up of stocks in a universe of interest. The analyst chooses which particular benchmark to use. For our purposes, a benchmark that summarizes the performance of managers, stocks, or groups specific to a universe of interest is best. There are at least several ways to do this. One is to treat the benchmark as a portfolio comprised of the elements under analysis. The performance of the benchmark is tracked by periodically determining the total value of the portfolio. The drawback to this

method is that, although portfolio elements are initially equally weighted, over time the influence of better performing elements will begin to dominate benchmark results as their values grow, while the influence of weaker elements on benchmark performance will diminish as their values stall or shrink. It is intuitively more attractive, and ultimately more practical, to periodically rebalance the benchmark. This is easily accomplished by summing the average periodic changes of elements in the selected universe. Alternatively, the sum of median periodic changes may be used.

2. Stocks in this study:

AA	BDX	DBD	GT	JCI	MAT	NTRS	PRX	SWK	USB
AAPL	BMS	DCI	HAL	JCP	MCD	NUE	PVH	T	UTX
ACXM	BP	DDS	HAS	JPM	MDR	NWL	QSII	TAP	UVV
ADM	BRS	DE	HD	JWN	MDT	NYT	R	TDW	VFC
ADP	CAG	DIS	HL	K	MGA	OII	RHI	TGT	VMC
AEP	CAR	DOV	HNZ	KEY	MHP	OLN	RJF	THC	VMI
AET	CASY	DOW	HPQ	KGC	MMM	OMX	ROK	THO	VZ
AFL	CAT	EAT	HRB	KLAC	MO	ORI	RRD	TKR	WAG
AIG	CBE	ECL	HRL	KO	MOLX	OSG	RSH	TM	WFSL
ALK	CDE	ELN	HSY	LEG	MRK	OXY	RYL	TMK	WHR
AMAT	CHD	ELX	IBM	LEN	MU	PAYX	SEIC	TSN	WMB
AMD	CINF	EMR	IDCC	LIZ	MUR	PBI	SLB	TTC	WMS
AMGN	CL	ERIC	IGT	LLY	MYL	PCAR	SLM	TXI	WMT
ASH	CLF	EXPD	INTC	LNC	NBL	PCH	SNA	TXT	WPO
ATO	CLX	F	IP	LOW	NBR	PCP	SNE	UIS	WSM
AVP	CMCSA	FDX	IPG	LPX	NEM	PEG	SO	UL	WTR
AXP	CSC	GCI	IR	LSI	NEU	PFE	SON	UN	WY
BA	CSX	GLW	IRF	LTD	NFG	PG	STJ	UNH	XOM
BAC	CTB	GNTX	ITW	LUV	NKE	PH	STR	UNP	XRX
BAX	CVS	GPC	JBHT	MAS	NOC	PIR	SVU	UNT	ZION

CHAPTER 3

Feedback and Capital Flow

O body swayed to music, O brightening glance, How can we know the dancer from the dance?

—W. B. Yeats, "Among School Children"

It was near sunset many years ago when I saw hundreds of small birds hovering in mid-air. They moved in unison, veering in one direction then another, rising then suddenly swooping. From a distance the flock took on the aspect of a single creature lumbering through the evening sky. I had never seen anything like it. What fascinated me was that each bird responded instantly to what appeared to be the random movement of the whole flock. How do they do it? I wondered. How do they communicate the next move? Is there a lead bird or some signal beyond my seeing or hearing?

That aerial dance, it is clear to me now, resulted from the interplay of positive and negative feedback as each bird responded to the movement of other birds, at once trying to keep up with the flock while at the same time avoiding collisions.

The dialectic of attraction and repulsion is a description of dynamic movement that produces emergent qualities on higher levels of organization.
—*Christian Fuchs*[1]

In 1986, Craig Reynolds developed Boids, a computer program that simulates the flocking of birds. Flocking is a particularly instructive case of emergence, in which, as Reynolds found, complex global behavior arises from the interplay of just a few simple rules. To create lifelike flocking behavior, Reynolds needed only three steering commands:

Cohesion—steer toward the average position of surrounding flockmates.
Alignment—steer toward the average heading of local boids.
Separation—steer away from nearest neighbors to avoid collisions.[2]

The first two call for individual boids to imitate the behavior of the flock, while the third requires that each boid avoid the flock by steering away from nearby flockmates. Complex flocking behavior, then, may be adequately depicted as the interaction of two distinct dynamics: attraction and repulsion. "Natural flocks seem to consist of two balanced, opposing behaviors: a desire to stay close to the flock and a desire to avoid collisions within the flock."[3]

Feedback

Traders, too, enter into a kind of dance, choreographed by attraction and repulsion. The operative dynamic is feedback.

Feedback is commonplace. Businesses routinely solicit feedback from customers, and that information returns to the marketplace in the form of improved products and services. The best companies seek feedback continuously, and in the process convert information into long-term success. To a large extent such feedback determines winners and losers and, more generally, helps move the economy forward. In a free-market society feedback is pervasive, so it should come as no surprise that feedback is at work in the equity market as well.

There are two sorts of feedback—positive and negative. A common example of positive feedback is the audio screech that occurs when a microphone gets too close to a speaker. Sound from the speaker is picked up by the microphone, then amplified and sent back through the speaker. Sound continues to loop through the system, and with each pass the volume increases until the limit of the amplifier is reached. All of this happens quickly, and the effect is both loud and annoying.

Another, less common example of positive feedback is a nuclear chain reaction, in which particles released from one area of nuclear material spark the release of a greater number of particles from areas nearby. The process accelerates rapidly until the whole mass is involved. The result is explosive.

A spreading fire is another example. A discarded match ignites the carpet. The fire spreads to the curtain, then up the wall. Quickly the whole room is in flames, and soon the entire house is burning.

In each of these cases, an accelerating trend continues until the limit of the system is reached. The amplifier peaks out, the nuclear material is spent, or all nearby fuel in the house burns up. Positive feedback exhibits an accelerating trend (see Figure 3.1) that, if allowed to run unchecked, persists until system resources are exhausted.

A good example of negative feedback is the thermostat, which cools a room as ambient temperature rises and heats as temperature falls. The thermostat stabilizes room temperature within a comfortable zone. Another example of negative feedback is the engine governor, commonly used to stabilize the output of industrial machinery.

An interesting example of negative feedback is the predator–prey relationship. An increase in the predator population puts pressure on the prey population. However, a fall in the number of available prey reduces the number of predators that may feed successfully, and so the predator population declines. A decline in predators, in turn, boosts the prey population,

FIGURE 3.1 Positive Feedback

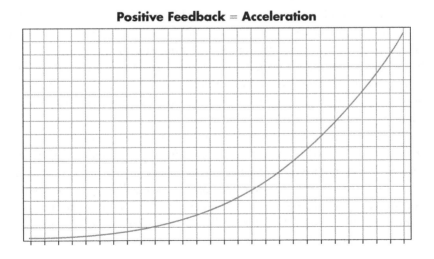

Positive Feedback = Acceleration

FIGURE 3.2 Negative Feedback

Negative Feedback = Stable (Cycle)

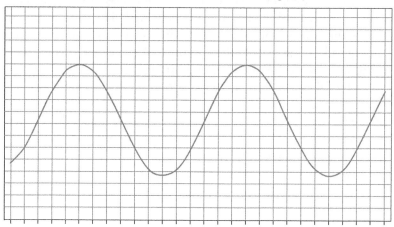

and so on. The interaction of predator and prey tends to stabilize both populations. Negative-feedback systems are stable (see Figure 3.2), with values fluctuating within a narrow range.

When traders respond to market events, they are closing a feedback loop. The actions of individual traders collect to produce changes in the market, and those changes prompt a collective response. In the case of positive feedback during an advancing market, rising prices trigger more buying on the part of the aggregate trader. Net buying lifts prices, and higher prices in turn prompt still more buying. An accelerating advance results. Positive feedback in a falling market, on the other hand, develops when falling prices induce traders to sell. Net selling pushes prices down, and lower prices encourage more selling. The result is an accelerating decline. Positive feedback, when it occurs, generates a trend. Traders' behavior during these periods may be characterized as "trend-following" (see Figure 3.3).

At other times, the reverse is true. Traders then trade against the crowd, and feedback between market inputs and traders' aggregate response turns negative. When negative feedback prevails, the composite trader reacts to rising prices by taking profits. Net selling puts pressure on prices. However, falling prices encourage traders to hunt for bargains among depressed issues. Bids for weakened stocks lift prices, and the cycle repeats (see Figure 3.4).

FIGURE 3.3 Positive Feedback

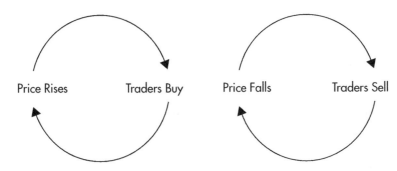

FIGURE 3.4 Negative Feedback

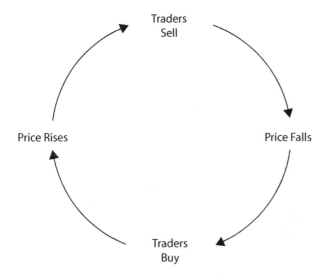

During periods when traders' behavior is primarily contrarian, negative feedback drives traders' response to price change, and price action tends to be either corrective or confined within a range.

Feedback and Capital Flow

Capital moves from one account to another in thousands of transactions daily, and each transaction adds energy to global capital flows. Since no individual trader is able to control capital flows, profits are earned only by properly navigating those currents.

The course of capital is determined by feedback. During periods when traders' response to price change is characterized by positive feedback, traders are inclined to sell into weakness and to buy into strength. As a result, capital flows out of weaker issues and into those that are stronger. This is true whether the overall market is rising or falling. Figure 3.5 pictures the flow of capital from weak targets SE of the benchmark equivalence line (BEL) into stronger targets NW of the BEL.

When feedback is positive, capital pumped into strong targets improves the relative strength of issues NW of the BEL. As relative strength improves, strong issues migrate further toward the NW. Laggards, on the other hand, come under selling pressure. As capital is drained from laggards, issues SE of the BEL become even weaker. Positive feedback in both rising and falling

FIGURE 3.5   Capital Flow during Periods of Positive Feedback

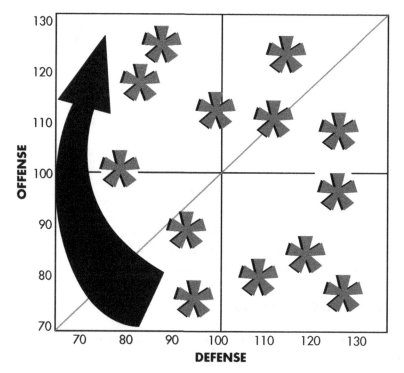

markets produces a northwesterly flow of capital and causes the universe to expand (see Figure 3.6).

During periods of negative feedback, capital flow across the BEL is reversed. In the aggregate, traders have turned from trend following to contrarian behavior. Contrarian traders offer stocks that are relatively strong and bid for relative-performance laggards. As a result, capital flows out of stronger issues and into weaker issues (see Figure 3.7).

Driven by negative feedback, targets that have been strong lose capital and retreat back towards the BEL, while targets with a recent history of weakness, impelled by infusions of new capital, move in a northwesterly direction. Both strong and weak targets migrate toward the BEL as negative feedback contracts the universe (see Figure 3.8).

The next set of charts records the relative performance of 151 industry groups.[4] Relative strength is computed using daily data over a six-month look-back. The first snapshot was taken in October 1998. After rallying early in the

FIGURE 3.6 Positive Feedback Expands the Universe

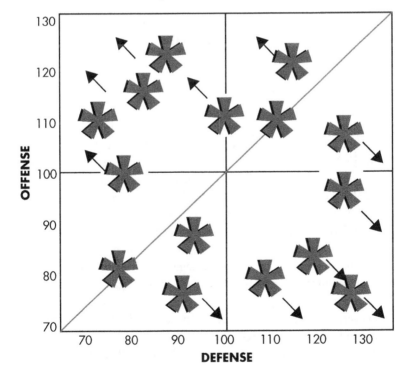

FIGURE 3.7   Capital Flow during Periods of Negative Feedback

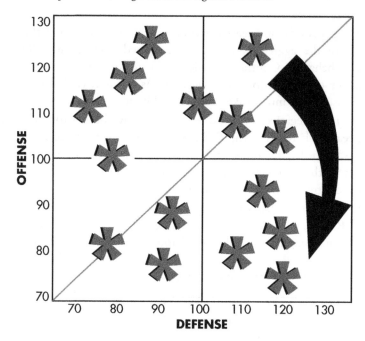

year, the market corrected under contrarian influence. The universe contracted, and groups aligned themselves along the BEL. This is a picture of the market at rest. The major differences to be detected are based on volatility, not on relative strength. Then, refreshed after a period of indolence, the market reached for new highs in November 1999 as bullish traders bid strong groups to extremes of relative strength. Laggards rallied, but not as well as the average group, and so drifted further SE of the BEL. As a result, the distance (or spread) between the strongest and weakest groups widened (see Figure 3.9).

The next three charts complete another episode of expansion and contraction. After peaking in the year 2000, the market corrected during 2001. Bids for stronger stocks were relaxed as laggards picked up relative support. The universe contracted, and by December, groups again huddled along the BEL (see Figure 3.10 on page 36).

However, the market's decline soon resumed, this time with more urgency. Traders shed or shorted weak groups most aggressively, and by June 2002, the weakest groups were far to the SE of the BEL (see Figure 3.11).

FIGURE 3.8 Negative Feedback Contracts the Universe

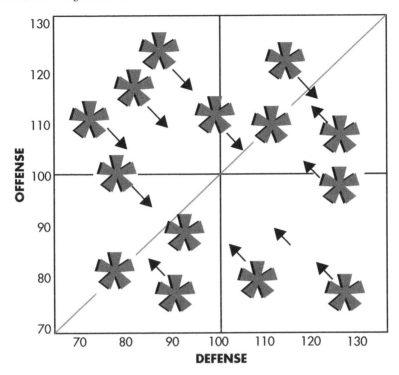

FIGURE 3.9 Positive Feedback Expands the Universe

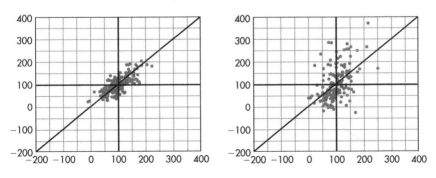

FIGURE 3.10 Negative Feedback Contracts the Universe

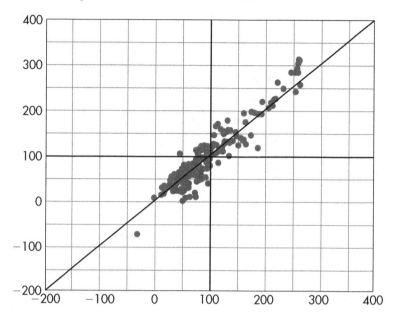

FIGURE 3.11 June 2002

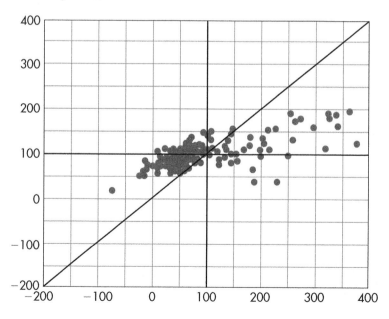

FIGURE 3.12 December 2002

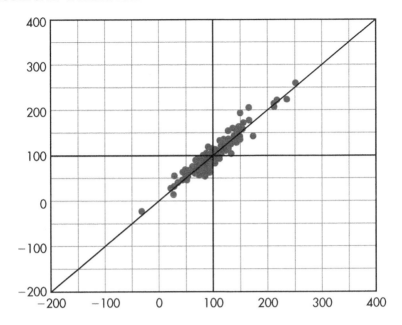

Now bearish, trend followers widened the spread between the strongest and weakest groups.

The market made an initial low in the summer of 2002, and by December, groups had been consolidating for six months. Differences based on relative strength narrowed as negative feedback held both stronger and weaker groups within a narrow range. Once more at rest, groups lined up along the BEL (Figure 3.12).

Calculating Relative Strength

To determine whether the universe of trading targets is expanding or contracting, the relative strength (RS) of each target in the universe must first be calculated. To compute RS, a little geometry is required. From the target's position in the northwest quadrant of the matrix (see Figure 3.13), I have drawn a square with NE and SW corners anchored on the BEL. Diagonal C is the hypotenuse of triangle ABC. A is equal to the target's offensive score

FIGURE 3.13   The Calculation of Relative Strength

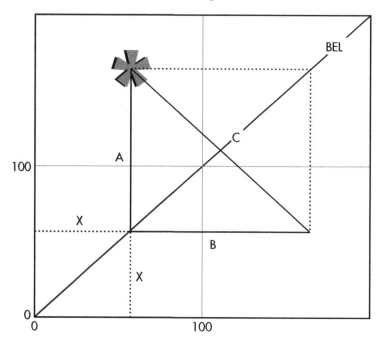

minus X, the target's defensive score. A and B are equal. Since we know the lengths of A and B, the value of C is determined from the Pythagorean theorem, $A^2 + B^2 = C^2$. The target's relative strength is measured as its distance from the BEL, or one-half of C. The formula for the absolute value of RS is:

$$\frac{\sqrt{A^2 + B^2}}{2}$$

If the offensive score is greater than the defensive score, then the target lies to the NW of the BEL and RS is positive; otherwise RS is negative.

The formula for calculating RS (the distance of a target from the BEL), may be reduced to a simpler form: RS = (Offensive Score − Defensive Score)/$\sqrt{2}$. The sign of RS is assigned as part of the formula.[5]

The Relative Strength Spread

The relative strength spread (RSS) is the gap between the average RS of those targets nearest the NW edge of the universe and the average RS of the weakest targets near the SE frontier (see Figure 3.14).

The next study of 200 stocks offers a running account of the average RS of both the strongest and weakest 10 percent of that universe from late 1998 through early 2003 (Figure 3.15).[6] The RS of strong stocks is always positive, while that of laggards is negative. The BEL, which separates strong from weak targets, is zero. The gap between the two, or the relative strength spread (RSS), varies over time with variations in the relative strength of leaders and laggards.

To calculate the RSS, the average RS of the weakest stocks in the universe is subtracted from the average RS of the strongest. Figure 3.16 shows the gap,

FIGURE 3.14 The Relative Strength Spread

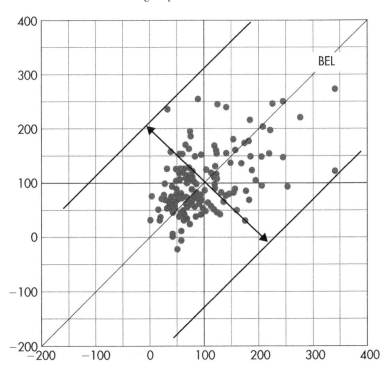

FIGURE 3.15 Relative Strength Leaders and Laggards

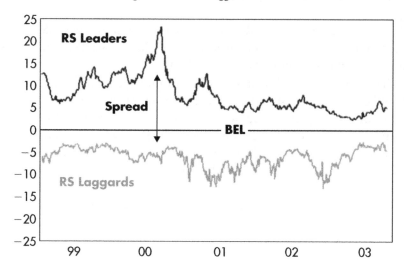

FIGURE 3.16 The Relative Strength Spread

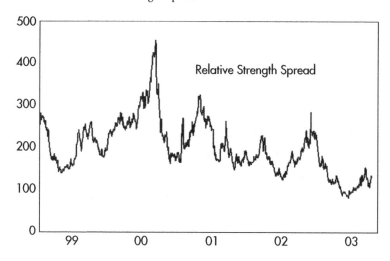

or spread, between the strongest and weakest 10 percent of stocks in the 200-stock universe.

The generally rising trend of the RSS from late 1998 through early 2000 indicates that the universe of stocks expanded throughout a long positive-feedback cycle. Except for a brief period during the spring of 1999, an advancing spread attests traders' confidence in the trend, which was then bullish. By early 2000, however, traders' enthusiasm was exhausted, and despite a continuing rally in the broad indexes, traders' aggregate behavior turned risk averse and contrarian. The spread pitched over, a sign that the market's dynamic had shifted from positive to negative feedback.

Trend Followers and Contrarians

Investing is an intellectual arms race.

—*Andrew B. Weisman*[7]

A heuristic is a set of rules, an abbreviated but workable model built from less-than-perfect information, employed as a practical guide for action. In practice, both trend following and contrarian methods encompass more or less well-defined heuristics with long histories, as George Chestnutt acknowledged in 1965.

> The principle of measuring the strength of a stock in relation to a market average has been in use for many years. I began experimenting with relative performance ratios in the early thirties. The best stock market technicians of that era had been using them for at least a generation before.[8]

One of the earliest formal studies of RS is Robert A. Levy's groundbreaking book, *The Relative Strength Concept of Common Stock Price Forecasting*, published in the 1968. Levy concluded that "the historically strongest stocks produced the best future results and the historically weakest stocks produced the worst."[9]

Levy and others uncovered a statistically significant relationship between a history of relative performance and future returns. Levy found that stocks showing superior RS over a six-month period produced better-than-benchmark results over the following six months, though shorter look-back periods produced positive results as well. Narasimhan Jegadeesh and Sheridan Titman echoed these conclusions. Their work showed that relative performance look-back periods of up to 12 months provided better-than-average forward returns.[10]

Perhaps as a result of these and later studies that drew similar conclusions, heuristic models employing relative performance have gained wide acceptance.

A recent study of European money managers found that although few managers surveyed relied exclusively on a single method, preferences were roughly evenly divided among three strategic options: trend following, contrarian, and buy and hold.[11]

Another study concluded that domestic fund managers "tend to buy stocks based on their past returns." Of the funds surveyed, a large majority (119) employed trend-following methods, while a significant but much smaller group (36) relied on contrarian strategies.[12]

While contrarians and trend followers subscribe to different heuristic models, both models are similar in that each offers rules intended to guide traders' response to market conditions. Each is a manual for feedback.

Notes

1. Christian Fuchs, "The Self-Organization of Matter," *Nature, Society, and Thought* 16, no. 3 (2003).
2. Craig W. Reynolds, "Flocks, Herds and Schools: A Distributed Behavioral Model," *Computer Graphics* 21, no. 4 (July 1987).
3. Ibid.
4. Morningstar groups in this study were accessed through Worden's TC2000:

MG111 MG312 MG333 MG425 MG522 MG628 MG722 MG742 MG811 MG833

MG113 MG313 MG334 MG431 MG523 MG629 MG723 MG747 MG812 MG834

MG114 MG314 MG341 MG432 MG525 MG631 MG724 MG761 MG813 MG835

MG121 MG315 MG342 MG433 MG526 MG632 MG726 MG762 MG814 MG836

MG122 MG316 MG343 MG434 MG527 MG633 MG727 MG763 MG815 MG837

MG123 MG317 MG344 MG441 MG529 MG634 MG728 MG764 MG816 MG838

MG124 MG321 MG345 MG448 MG611 MG635 MG729 MG765 MG822 MG841

MG125 MG322 MG346 MG511 MG612 MG636 MG731 MG766 MG823 MG842

MG126 MG323 MG349 MG512 MG621 MG638 MG732 MG767 MG824 MG843

MG131 MG324 MG351 MG513 MG622 MG712 MG733 MG771 MG825 MG845

MG133 MG325 MG411 MG514 MG623 MG713 MG734 MG772 MG826 MG847

MG134 MG326 MG414 MG515 MG624 MG714 MG735 MG774 MG827 MG853

MG135 MG327 MG419 MG516 MG625 MG715 MG736 MG775 MG828 MG912

MG136 MG331 MG421 MG517 MG626 MG717 MG737 MG776 MG831 MG913

MG311 MG332 MG423 MG521 MG627 MG721 MG739 MG777 MG832 MG914

MG915

5. Since A = (Offense − Defense) and B = (Offense − Defense), then

$$RS = \frac{\sqrt{\left((\text{Offense} - \text{Defense})^2 + (\text{Offense} - \text{Defense})^2\right)}}{2}$$

$$RS = \frac{\sqrt{\left(2 \times (\text{Offense} - \text{Defense})^2\right)}}{2}$$

$$RS = \frac{\sqrt{2 \times \left((\text{Offense} - \text{Defense})^2\right)}}{2}$$

$$RS = \frac{\sqrt{2} \times (\text{Offense} - \text{Defense})}{2}$$

$$RS = \frac{(\text{Offense} - \text{Defense})}{\sqrt{2}}$$

6. For a list of the stocks, see Chapter 2, endnote 2.
7. Andrew B. Weisman, in *How I Became a Quant*, eds. Richard R. Lindsey and Barry Schachter (Hoboken, NJ: John Wiley & Sons, 2007).
8. George Chestnutt, *Stock Market Analysis: Facts and Principles* (New York: American Investors Corp, 1965).
9. Robert A. Levy, *The Relative Strength Concept of Common Stock Price Forecasting* (New York: Investors' Fund, 1968).
10. Narasimhan Jegadeesh and Sheridan Titman, "Returns to Buying and Selling Losers: Implications for Stock Market Efficiency," *Journal of Finance* (March, 1993).

11. Torsten Brozynski, Lukas Menkhoff, and Ulrich Schmidt, "The Use of Momentum, Contrarian and Buy-&-Hold Strategies: Survey Evidence from Fund Managers," University of Hannover (December 2003).

12. Mark Grinblatt, Sheridan Titman, and Russ Wermers, "Momentum Investment Strategies, Portfolio Performance and Herding," *American Economic Review* (December 1995).

CHAPTER 4

The Janus Factor

There are two kinds of people in the world—those who divide everything in the world into two kinds of things and those who don't.

—Kenneth Boulding[1]

My desk is a mess again. Papers and books are strewn about, and the piles grow daily. The clutter is getting to me, and, frankly, it's hard to think in an organized way with so much disorganization about. I know that sooner or later I will get to the task of putting books back on the shelf and filing papers, but it's an expense of effort and time I find too easy to put off.

And so it goes. My desk, the yard, my own body all demand effort and energy from me if they are not to fall into disrepair. At times it seems as if life amounts to nothing more than maintenance against the everyday tendency of things to run down. Against this tendency, living beings harness energy to restore order out of disorder. Life itself depends on the energy that emanates beyond the biosphere, from deep within the sun. Without that source, all life on earth would become extinct, the atmosphere would cease to roil, and the landscape turn to an inert, cold desert where nothing moves.

> **en•tro•py:** the tendency for all matter and energy in the universe to evolve toward a state of inert uniformity; the inevitable and steady deterioration of a system or society.[2]

Entropy is the propensity for things to decay, to move toward disarray, disorder and degeneration. The notion of entropy covers "the degree of uncertainty or disorganization of a system."[3] Not just life, but all sorts of ordered systems fall prey to entropy.

Structure and Entropy

The most fundamental concept in cybernetics is that of "difference," either that two things are recognizably different or that one thing has changed with time.

—*W. Ross Ashby*[4]

The prime mover in a financial market is not value or price, but price differences: not averaging, but arbitraging.

—*Benoit Mandelbrot*[5]

All structure involves differentiation. One note played over and over is noise, not music. However, play one note, then another, and sound becomes something more. The structure of music emerges in the space between the notes, in their difference. An office tower is a monument to differentiation. The common stuff of earth is separated, refined, and shaped into distinct structures, which are ultimately joined to create an even grander structure.

When traders exhibit trend-following behavior, positive feedback widens performance differences among groups. This process may be viewed as an evolution toward increased structure. Since the creation of any structure requires energy, positive feedback is a dynamic that injects energy into the market. When traders turn contrarian, however, the opposite effect is seen. Strong groups are offered and weaker groups receive a bid. As stronger and weaker groups migrate toward the benchmark, structures built up during the process of differentiation collapse, and energy dissipates.

A new deck of cards is structured by suit and rank. Dealt a fresh deck, even untutored players can beat the dealer. Because shuffling reduces structure and increases randomness, or entropy, decks are routinely shuffled during games of chance in order to eliminate any advantage to card counters.[6]

An increase in entropy entails loss of information embedded in structure. As groups converge towards the benchmark, critical information stored as differences in relative strength (RS) dissipates until there is little perceived benefit to picking one group over another. This is just the situation one faces in a game of chance when presented with more or less equally likely alternatives. For the trend follower, trading during entropic periods amounts to placing bets without sufficient information, without an edge.

Any relative strength strategy is based on advantages offered by structure. When positive feedback expands the universe, new structures based on RS emerge from the randomized pile left after the most-recent period of contraction. Since reorganization of the market takes time, traders are able to profit by recognizing increasing differentiation among industry groups in time to place bets. The emergence of structure is the trend.

The place of greatest meaning hovers exactly between order and randomness.

—*J. R. Pierce*[7]

The battle line is constantly drawn and redrawn between two competing paradigms, one pushing the system toward regeneration and structure and the other pulling conditions back toward entropy and equilibrium. The market exists at the boundary between opposed forces driving positive and negative feedback.

Confidence

Consider the following game. A deck of cards is revealed one at a time. Participants are invited to bet on the next card. Here is the first series drawn: King of Spades, Three of Diamonds, Jack of Diamonds, Ten of Hearts, Two of Clubs, Seven of Hearts. What is the next card? Stumped? Would any bet make sense?

Here is the second series: Ace of Spades, King of Spades, Queen of Spades, Jack of Spades, Ten of Spades, Nine of Spades. Having recognized the structure of a fresh deck, one might venture a bet on the next card in the series with some confidence. If the Eight of Spades is drawn, expectations are met, and confidence grows.

Of course, we can't measure traders' confidence directly in a price-based system, but if we are to speculate about traders' motivations at all, then confidence is a disposition that fits the facts nicely. Confidence in this context may be seen as the progressive confirmation of expectations. Expectations adapt to fit recent experience, and as expectations are confirmed, confidence is rewarded. Increasing confidence encourages traders to pursue risk. When traders exhibit sufficient confidence to defer profits and chase strong stocks into new high ground, trends develop and accelerate, and profits for those trading with the trend come easily. Alternatively, the aggregate trader demonstrates confidence in declining prices by liquidating the weakest stocks. Price direction is then durable, albeit negative, and traders benefit by selling into weakness. In either case, the controlling dynamic is positive feedback. Traders' expectations are confirmed, and confidence in the direction of price is evidenced by trend-following behavior.

At some point, however, expectations are not met, and once traders lose confidence in the immediate direction of price, the dynamic changes. Now risk averse and contrarian, traders in the aggregate trim back trading commitments, or take profits quickly in stocks that have rallied and instead focus bids on fallen laggards. When the controlling dynamic is negative feedback, traders' expectations are lowered, price trends are short-lived, and profits become elusive.

Is the Market Predictable?

More zeal and energy, more fanatical hope, and more intense anguish have been expended over the past century in efforts to "forecast" the stock market than in almost any other single line of human action.

—*Richard Dana Skinner*[8]

It's a cultural thing. By the time the calendar turns to a new year, the ritual of soothsaying is in full swing. Market commentators feel no small pressure to peer into the mist and tell what they see in the year ahead. To call the results of such efforts nonsense is too harsh. Much good thought by many bright and well-informed people goes into these new-year prognostications. But they end up mostly wrong anyway. Some, of course, turn out to be right, but the problem is that the rest of us cannot know which forecast is accurate until it is too late to make the trade. So even the best—or luckiest— prediction is not of much use. It is unlikely that we can trump market risk through prediction, since a prediction is a prediction just because it can be wrong. Prediction free of risk is not prediction but omniscience.

Markets aside, the predictable routine of most of our days is comforting. We know, or think we know, what to expect. Still, we make sure that our fire and health insurance policies are paid. After all, some things are more predictable than others. The sun will surely rise tomorrow, but it is winter in the Northwest as I write, and I cannot say with any certainty when the sun will make its next appearance.

Throw a die, and the result is unpredictable, a matter of chance. Or is it? Most of us believe that one thing determines the next in a linear, if sometimes hidden, chain of cause and effect. If we could calculate the velocity of the die and the angle of flight, if we could measure the impact of the die on the table—if these physical factors and more could be taken into account, then surely we should be able to predict which number will end right-side up.

Theoretically, maybe, but not in the real world of dice and crap tables. The analysis of physical systems, such as the toss of a die, can be overwhelmingly complicated. Social systems push complication to yet another level: complexity. As a characterization of complex systems, the linear paradigm so successfully applied to physical systems comes up short because social systems introduce something novel: goal-seeking agents.

He intends only his own gain, and he is in this, as in many other cases, led by an invisible hand to promote an end which was not part of his intention.
—*Adam Smith*[9]

The market is the sum of countless independent agents, each seeking "only his own gain." Nevertheless, the market does not dissolve into chaos, but is a coherent system that self-organizes around the common pursuit of profit. A simple example of self-organization is the behavior of pedestrians as they cross at an intersection. In Figure 4.1, two sets of pedestrians gather at either side of a busy boulevard, waiting for the light to change. Once the light turns green, pedestrians begin walking in opposite directions. There is some hesitation and even disorder as those in the lead from one side of the street encounter those from the other side. Lead walkers step to the right or to the left to make room for opposing traffic, and other pedestrians, seeing that a way through has been established, follow behind. Very quickly traffic separates into alternating rows passing in opposite directions (see Figure 4.2).

FIGURE 4.1 Pedestrians Gather

FIGURE 4.2 Pedestrians Cross

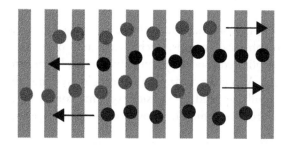

Pedestrians spontaneously organize themselves in a way that efficiently meets the shared goal of getting to the other side of the street. Remarkably, all of this happens without the benefit of planning or oversight by a traffic director. The number of rows and the precise pattern vary from crossing to crossing. In one case pedestrians form three queues and in another two or four, which pass either to the left or to the right. The tendency of pedestrians to separate into well-defined queues increases as the density of the crowd, and thus pressure to find a way through, increases.

A pedestrian's skill set is modest and, fortunately, need not include the ability to predict traffic patterns. It is enough to recognize and adapt to immediate pressures. From the pedestrian's point of view, the predictability of the system is not an issue.

Now imagine a group of academics standing by with clipboards and stopwatches. Their task is to develop a theory that accounts for pedestrians' behavior under varying conditions. The theory they come up with will be judged successful only if its predictions prove correct. In this case, predictability is not just an issue; it is *the* issue.

Suppose further that, after talking to systems analysts, our pedestrians become convinced that in order to find a way to the other side of the street, each must first successfully predict which pattern, out of a range of options, the group will form. What had been a straightforward process becomes a daunting problem.

Making predictions is appropriate in some contexts, but not in all. Insisting that the predictive methods so successfully employed in science apply as well to trading blurs rather than clarifies important distinctions between the two pursuits, a point driven home by Bernard Baruch's quip, "If all you have is a hammer, everything looks like a nail."

Still, shouldn't the flow of traffic be predictable, at least in theory? Since the system is made up of individuals, we should be able to predict the overall pattern of traffic by first predicting the outcome of forces acting on each pedestrian before adding up the paths of individual pedestrians to arrive at our prediction for the whole. But we can't. Pedestrians' trajectory toward self-organization is influenced not only by outside forces such as vehicle traffic, the condition of the street and traffic lights, weather, and so on, but also by the reactions of individual pedestrians to the collective actions of the crowd of which they are a part. The logic of crossing the street is circular, not linear. Such reflexivity moves street crossing beyond the merely complicated to the complex. In complex systems, analysis that attempts to reduce the behavior of the whole to the independent behavior of its parts offers no insight, and predictability, which is a feature of linear systems, fades.

The circular logic of self-organization may magnify or dampen emerging patterns in ways that cannot be anticipated. Surprise is a feature of complex systems. This dynamic runs counter to the mechanistic paradigm, which assumes a linear, proportional, and, therefore, predictable relationship between cause and effect (the more I turn the radio's volume control, the louder the music). Even when initial conditions and transformation rules are known, the reflexivity of self-organizing systems makes predicting global behavior futile.

Successful investing is anticipating the anticipation of others.

—*J. M. Keynes*[10]

J. M. Keynes famously compared the market to a newspaper contest in which competitors are asked to choose the six most beautiful women among photos of a hundred. Entrants win a prize if their selections match or come closest to the six receiving the most votes. The bet, then, is not which woman is most beautiful, but which will, on average, be thought most beautiful by the contestants. Anyone serious about winning would not pick his own favorites, but would try to predict which photos will garner the most votes. The task immediately becomes convoluted, as Keynes points out:

> It is not a case of choosing those that, to the best of one's judgment, are really the prettiest, nor even those that average opinion genuinely thinks the prettiest. We have reached the third degree where we devote our intelligences to anticipating what average opinion expects the average opinion to be. And there are some, I believe, who practice the fourth, fifth and higher degrees.[11]

The logic of Keynes's beauty contest lifts simpler forms of complex self-organization, like crossing the street, to a higher level of complexity by introducing competition. Competition triggers iterative degrees of second-guessing. Keynes concludes that just as the contest does not decide which woman is most beautiful, but, rather, which is thought to be most beautiful, markets do not advance the best stocks, but only those thought to be the best, or thought to be thought the best, and so on.

When agents in a self-organizing system are competitors, predictability suffers a near-fatal blow. If the play of some competitors is too regular, other players exploit recurring patterns of play. Predictability becomes a disadvantage. Competitive pressures tend to push self-organizing systems toward novelty and, hence, unpredictability.

Most social activity is goal seeking, not truth seeking. In complex systems, goal seeking prompts agents to search the space of possible solutions from one mode of organization to another in an attempt to maximize some value. Why did the trader cross the street? In search of profit. That search has been facilitated in recent years by the rise of computer-assisted algorithmic trading. Computers process vast amounts of data, and trading options are quickly calculated and weighed. Just as pedestrians go through an initial stage of disorder and confusion, emerging patterns may at first lack clear definition. Sensitive programs, however, pick up a trickle of profit and begin to commit capital. Like pedestrians taking the path of least resistance, other agents recognize an increasingly discernible pattern in the flow of capital and follow suit. Over a relatively short period, an emerging rule set becomes apparent as it attracts and is reinforced by new followers. It is traders' profit-driven self-organization, as spontaneous and unplanned as pedestrians' traffic patterns, which renders the market intelligible.

Intelligible, but not predictable. The predictability of linear systems assumes objectivity: The properties of the observer shall not enter the description of his observations. Such objectivity protects science from the bane of paradox. But in complex systems, individuals become both observers and the observed. Traders constantly respond to ever-changing *local* conditions (am I making/losing money?) as well as to evolving *global* states of the system (is the market up, down, flat, etc.), which their actions, in part, generate.

From the practical point of view of an analyst attempting to predict prices, it may be irrelevant whether the market is linear and complicated or reflexive and complex since both sorts of systems present difficulties that ultimately frustrate prediction. Nevertheless, market predictions are pervasive and will no doubt continue to be offered freely. That is natural and perhaps necessary to a functioning market system. Predictive activity is, after all, evidence of individuals' attention to the global state of the system, part of a feedback loop which tunes the actions of individual traders to the whole.

That market prices are not predictable may be considered heretical by some since, if taken seriously, the thesis shakes the philosophical ground under methodologies that attempt to forecast price. If traders are denied the ability to predict, how, then, can trading decisions be justified?

Charles Darwin observed, "It is not the strongest of the species that survives, nor the most intelligent, but the one most responsive to change."[12] Self-organizing systems are adaptive. The flow of pedestrians adapts to accommodate obstructions or other exogenous pressures without disintegrating. There are often a number of possible organized states around which pedestrians' goals may be achieved, though some may be better, or fitter, than others. The ability to adapt gets pedestrians safely across the street. Since the market is a complex social system, adaptive rather than predictive methods may lead to trading success as well.

When people are free to do as they please, they usually imitate each other.
—*Eric Hoffer*[13]

Evolutionary theory holds that individuals not well suited to environmental change are less likely to survive and to pass on their genes than are other, fitter variants. Biological adaptation, then, is a process of elimination.

Social adaptation, on the other hand, is a process of imitation. At the beginning of the twentieth century the French sociologist Gabriel Tarde observed, "The unvarying characteristic of every social fact whatsoever is that it is imitative."[14] An American contemporary of Tarde's, James Mark Baldwin, elaborates Tarde's theme:

> Imitation to the intelligent and earnest imitator is never slavish, never mere repetition; it is, on the contrary, *a means to further ends,* a method of absorbing what is present in others and of making it over in forms peculiar to one's own temper and valuable to one's own genius.
> —*James Mark Baldwin*[15]

Adept imitation, not prediction, is the key to successful trend following.

Balancing Acts and Paradigm Shifts

> What is opposite strives toward union, out of the diverse there arises the most beautiful harmony, and the struggle makes everything come about.
> —*Heraclitus*[16]

I was still a boy when I learned the trick of balancing a broomstick in the palm of my hand: If the broom begins to tip to one side, quickly move ahead of the falling stick to restore balance. When I perform this trick, there are moments when I experience a calm sense of mastery. But those moments do not last. I get into trouble when the broom begins to tilt, then oscillates more and more erratically. I feel myself losing control as the oscillations widen, and I'm likely to crash into a chair or a table as I lurch about, trying to prevent the broomstick from falling to the ground. A tilting broomstick is an example of positive feedback, which, if left unchecked, will tip the broom beyond the point of any recovery. Balance is restored only if negative feedback gets ahead of that process in time to stop the system from crashing.

Price discovery is a balancing act between forces of positive and negative feedback, one destabilizing, the other steadying. We may learn the dynamics of each, yet not divine when the market will tilt from one to the other, or why. That remains a mystery.

It is all so simple: the snow falls on the bamboo leaf, which gently bends under its weight: at a certain moment the snow slips to the ground without the leaf itself having stirred.

—Eugen Herrigel and Daisetz T. Suzuki[17]

Notes

1. Quoted in Gerald M. Weinberg, *An Introduction to General Systems Thinking* (New York: John Wiley & Sons, 1975).
2. *The American Heritage Dictionary.*
3. E. M. Rogers, *A History of Communication Study: A Biographical Approach* (The Free Press, 1994.)
4. W. Ross Ashby, *Introduction to Cybernetics* (New York: John Wiley & Sons, 1961).
5. Benoit Mandelbrot, *The (Mis)Behavior of Markets* (New York: Basic Books, 2004).
6. There is a trivial sense in which any arrangement of cards constitutes structure. But structure in that sense offers no information. Information implies some agreed upon convention which bestows meaning. Structures that carry information are always special cases, determined by convention.
7. J. R. Pierce, *Symbols, Signals, and Noise* (New York: Harper & Row, 1961).
8. Richard Dana Skinner, *Seven Kinds of Inflation* (New York: McGraw-Hill, 1937), 93.
9. Adam Smith, *Wealth of Nations* (London: W. Strahan and T. Cadell, 1776).
10. As quoted in Gregory Bergman, *Isms: From Autoerotism to Zoroastrianism—An Irreverent Guide* (Avon, MA: Adams Media, 2006), 105.
11. J. M. Keynes, *The General Theory of Employment, Interest and Money* (Cambridge, UK: Cambridge University Press, 1936).
12. Charles Darwin, *On the Origin of Species* (London: John Murray, 1859).
13. Eric Hoffer, *The Passionate State of Mind and Other Aphorisms* (New York: Joanna Cotler Books, 1955).
14. Gabriel Tarde, *The Laws of Imitation*, trans. Elsie Clews Parsons (New York: Henry Holt, 1903), 41.
15. James Mark Baldwin, *The Individual and Society* (Boston: Richard G. Badger, 1911), 36.
16. Heraclitus fragments, Diels-Kranz 22 B8.
17. Eugen Herrigel and Daisetz T. Suzuki, *Zen In the Art of Archery* (New York: Pantheon Books, 1953).

CHAPTER 5

Seasons of Success

In some seasons, trend following is good; in others, reversing is good. The problem is how to differentiate the two seasons in advance.
—Victor Niederhoffer, *The Education of a Speculator*[1]

Traders employ various methods to identify trades. Peter Brandt trades breakouts from recognizable chart patterns, while Paul Tudor Jones looks for contrarian turning points based on historical cycles and fundamentals. Some rely on experience and intuition while others employ more mechanical systems to rationalize trades. Nearly all the traders interviewed by Jack D. Schwager, however, attribute their long-term success not to some specific technique for identifying trades, but to wise money management. In his book *Diary of a Professional Commodities Trader*, Brandt makes it clear that trade management, not trade selection, is more important to success:

> Trade identification is the least important of all trading components. The trading process itself and risk management are much more crucial components to overall success in trading operations.[2]

Gary Biefelt sums up trade management as "staying with your winners and getting rid of your losers."[3] Regardless of the method used to trigger a trade, successful traders judge a position by only one standard once the trade has been taken: Is it working? If forward profitability is the criterion by which an existing trade is evaluated, then why not apply the same test to trade selection?

To find out whether a relative strength strategy is working, first the strongest and weakest stocks are identified as of day D, then the changes in each set are averaged and recorded as of the following day, or $D+1$. Forward changes for each set of stocks are cumulated. While the specific stocks that rank among the strongest and weakest may vary daily, this method provides continuous accounts of the forward performance of relative strength leaders and laggards.

The Venturi Effect

In Figure 5.1, relative strength (RS) leaders are limited to stocks among the strongest 10 percent, and RS laggards to the weakest 10 percent. Why 10 percent? Why not include a larger selection, say, the top and bottom 25 percent, or even the strongest and weakest halves of the universe? Typically, targets closest to the frontiers of the universe are more volatile. During bullish expansions, the best immediate gains are, therefore, likely to come from the strongest targets, those nearest the NW edge of expansion.[4] Similarly, during bearish expansions the best short profits come from the weakest stocks and groups.

Hold your thumb over a garden hose, and the velocity of the water spray increases as cross-sectional area decreases. Heightened volatility of groups and

FIGURE 5.1 Forward Performance of RS Leaders and Laggards

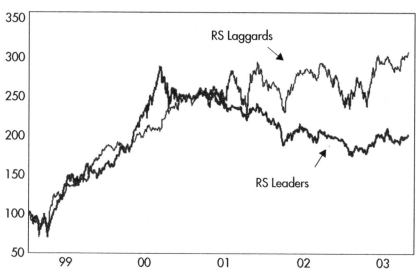

stocks near relative strength extremes may be due to a similar Venturi effect. As RS readings expand during advances, trend followers focus buying on a narrowing selection of the strongest stocks, creating greater buying pressure on fewer issues. Similarly, when prices fall under momentum, traders exert disproportionate selling pressure on the weakest groups and stocks.

To illustrate how the Venturi effect applies to trading, the next chart compares the forward performance of the strongest 20 stocks in our 200-stock universe to the average of the 20 stocks closest to the median RS. In all examples, relative strength was computed using daily data and a six-month look-back period. Figure 5.2 reveals that the strongest stocks rallied more than near-median stocks prior to the year 2000. Note that even when the universe began to contract under contrarian control after 2000, the volatility of the strongest stocks remains high, evidenced by the relative speed with which leading issues declined. We'll examine this period of contraction in more detail later in this chapter.

The forward returns of the 20 most-laggard stocks also exhibit greater velocity in both directions than that of near-median stocks (see Figure 5.3).[5]

Figure 5.4 summarizes five separate back-tests of long-short positions based on the immediate direction of the relative strength spread (RSS). The

FIGURE 5.2 Forward Performance of Strongest 10 Percent

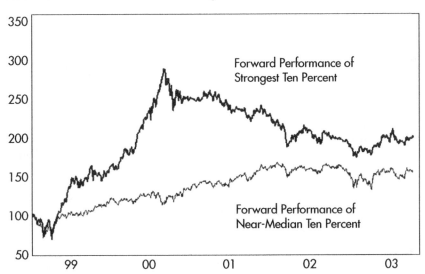

FIGURE 5.3   Forward Performance of Weakest 10 Percent

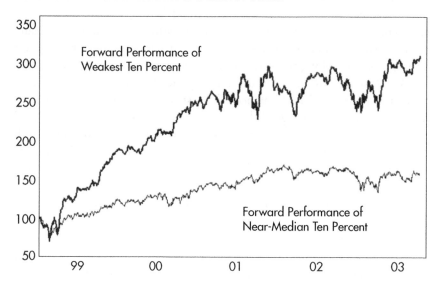

FIGURE 5.4   Long-Short Results versus 200-Stock Average

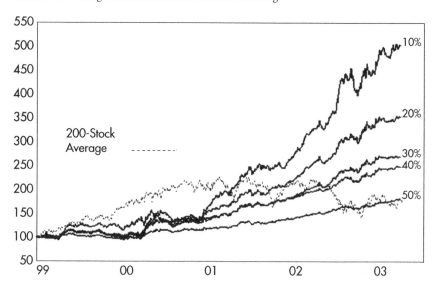

method employed is simple, direct, and free of any attempt to optimize outcomes. The RSS determines whether the universe of 200 stocks is expanding or contracting. On days when the RSS rises (universe expands), long positions are selected from relatively strong stocks, and short positions are selected from relatively weak stocks. Long-short positions are reversed when the RSS falls (universe contracts). Net one-day forward returns are cumulated. No leverage is assumed. No allowance is made for commissions or other costs.

The back-test was made assuming long/short stock sets of varying size; in Figure 5.4, "10%" tags the overall performance that results from trading only the strongest and the weakest 10 percent of the universe. That set posted a gain of 404 percent with a maximum drawdown of 14 percent. Over the same period (4.3 years), the 200-stock average gained 69 percent, with a maximum drawdown of 39 percent.

Set size was increased incrementally until the strong half of all stocks were positioned on one side of trades and the relatively weak half on the other (tagged "50%"). The best overall performance came from the 10 percent of stocks nearest the extremes of the universe. Test results are consistent with the Venturi effect and demonstrate the efficacy of the RSS.

The Relative Strength Spread and the Performance Spread

I refer to two versions of *spread* in the chapters that follow. The RSS measures the gap in relative strength between RS leaders and RS laggards. The performance spread measures the difference in cumulative forward performance between RS leaders and laggards. Like the RSS, the performance spread indicates positive feedback when rising and negative feedback when declining. Not surprisingly, since the performance spread (see Figure 5.5) and the relative strength spread (see Figure 5.6) both reflect feedback at work in the market, both are broadly in synch, and evidence of feedback provided by one is generally confirmed by the other. However, the performance spread offers information more immediately relevant to trade management, and by extension to trade selection, since it reveals whether relative-strength strategies are working.

Since the velocity of returns is highest near the boundaries of the universe, it is here that the struggle for control between trend followers and contrarians is most sensitively measured.[6] In Figure 5.5, the cumulative

FIGURE 5.5   Performance Spread

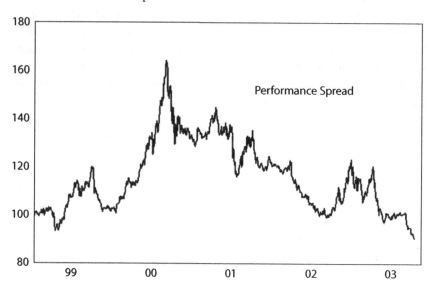

FIGURE 5.6   Relative Strength Spread

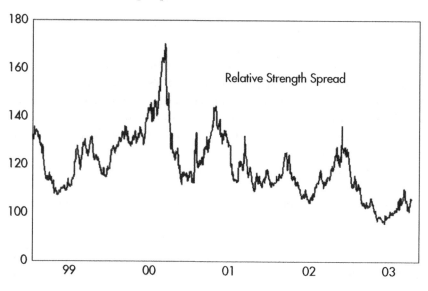

forward performance of the weakest 10 percent of stocks in the 200-stock universe is subtracted from that of the strongest 10 percent to produce the performance spread.

Both measures of feedback indicate traders' confidence in the trend. When traders exhibit confidence, both versions of the spread rise and above-average returns may be harvested at low risk by focusing selections near the extremes of RS. There are darker periods, however, when traders' confidence ebbs, as indicated by declines in the spreads. Volatile returns then converge, and risks for those trading with the trend are high.

The Performance Spread: 1998–2003

I've selected the period from 1998 to 2003 for examination because the effects of positive and negative feedback can be seen in both rising and falling markets. Figure 5.7 shows the forward performance of RS leaders and laggards as well as the performance spread. In the months leading up to 2000, positive feedback drove the market higher, traders exhibited confidence in the rally by bidding preferentially for the strongest stocks, and a strategy that favored longs in RS leaders did well. The performance spread reveals a

FIGURE 5.7 RS Leaders, RS Laggards, and Performance Spread

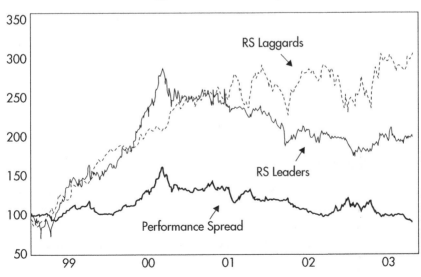

sudden and dramatic change in underlying dynamics in early 2000, however, as the series began to fall. Feedback turned negative, traders became risk averse, and a contrarian pattern of trading emerged. Laggards received the better bid, and profits were taken in stocks that had moved into positions of RS leadership.

The decline of the performance spread after March 2000 indicates traders' overall lack of confidence in the trends of both RS leaders and laggards. Price improvement met selling, while declines found support. Negative feedback was dominant over the next several years. As a result, the average stock in the universe carved out a broad trading range (see Figure 5.8).

FIGURE 5.8   Average Stock versus the Performance Spread

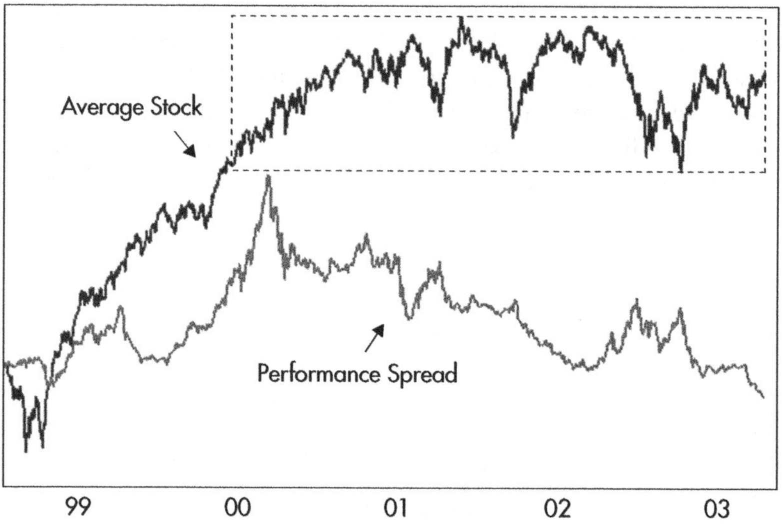

A Tour of Momentum

The charts in this section (Figures 5.9 through 5.12) focus on several specific momentum-driven episodes between late 1998 and the spring of 2001. As in a tour of Hollywood mansions, we will drive by some of the best examples of momentum and only occasionally pass through less-tony areas, those lacking momentum. All the sites along the way were selected after the fact, and the tour does not review the day-to-day decisions a trader would have faced any more than a tour of homes reveals the many decisions made by architects and buyers.

In the first chart (see Figure 5.9), RS leaders rallied well from November through early 1999, while RS laggards traded narrowly. A rising performance spread signaled a period of positive feedback that rewarded long positions in the strongest stocks. Prior to November, both leaders and laggards rallied, but a flat-to-declining performance spread indicates that the rally lacked the positive feedback that warrants trends.

FIGURE 5.9   October 1998 through January 1999

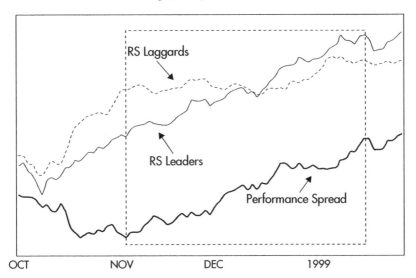

From mid-summer 1999 through the spring of 2000, traders again pursued strength, and the performance spread rose (see Figure 5.10). Both leaders and laggards rallied along with the spread. This is the profile of a market that leads to strength-following success. Then, in March, a sudden change in traders' mind-set, from trend-following enthusiasm to contrarian risk aversion, is signaled by a reversal of the performance spread. Though momentum had dissipated, the market continued to rally. Under the cover of

FIGURE 5.10   May 1999 through April 2000

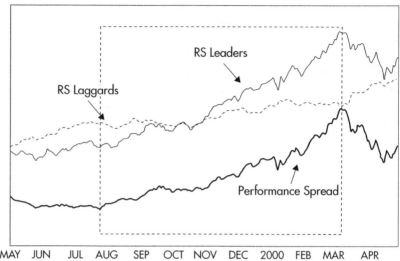

MAY JUN   JUL AUG   SEP   OCT NOV DEC 2000 FEB   MAR   APR

continuing strength in widely published indexes dominated by large-cap laggards, profits were taken in smaller-cap growth stocks that had led the previous advance.

Over the next several years, from early 2000 to 2003, the malaise of negative feedback was only occasionally interrupted by surges of positive feedback, all of which were attended by sinking prices. The first clear indication that traders had turned aggressively bearish came during a decline in September 2000, when positive feedback, indicated by an advancing performance spread, pushed laggards lower at a rate faster than that of declining leaders (see Figure 5.11). After the break earlier in the year, this was traders' initial opportunity to assume short positions backed by momentum. Note that once selling became exhausted in mid-October, contrarians took control by bidding up oversold laggards, at which point the market rallied as the spread declined. After a momentum-driven decline, simultaneous reversals in both price and the performance spread signal a corrective rally.

A rising spread put its imprimatur on another decline in early in 2001 (see Figure 5.12). Traders again demonstrated confidence in the decline by focusing offerings on the weakest stocks.

FIGURE 5.11 September 2000 through November 2000

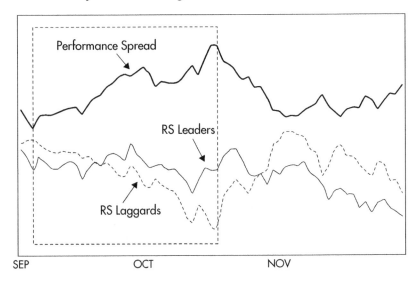

FIGURE 5.12 January 2001 through April 2001

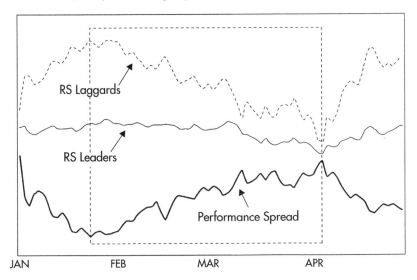

Group Studies

In their 1999 paper, "Do Industries Explain Momentum?," Tobias J. Moskowitz and Mark Grinblatt conclude that industry membership accounts for stock momentum and that "industry momentum strategies are more profitable than individual stock momentum strategies."

> The existence of industries as a key source of momentum profits may support the viability of behavioral models that have been offered for the individual stock momentum anomaly.[7]

The logic prompting traders to take action in a particular stock frequently applies as well to other stocks within the same industry or sector. Institutional investors commit large sums to industry themes, often more than can be easily accommodated by a single, or even a few, stocks. Substantial stakes may therefore require positions in a number of thematically related issues. For these reasons, a universe of industry group indexes may detect momentum as well or better than one made up of individual stocks. The analyses offered in the next two charts employ the universe of 151 Morningstar industry groups (see Chapter 3).

In the first chart (see Figure 5.13), a momentum-driven decline begins in May and persists until the market bottoms in early October.

FIGURE 5.13   Group Universe: March 2001 through November 2001

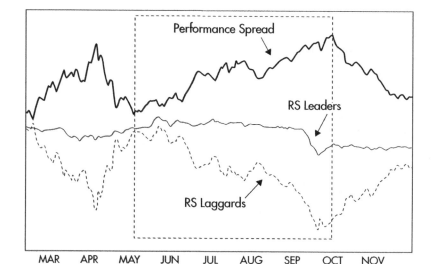

FIGURE 5.14 Group Universe: February 2002 through August 2002

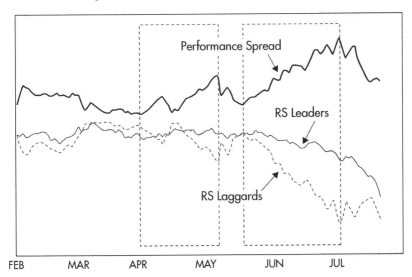

In Figure 5.14, a rising performance spread identifies the onset of a shorting opportunity in early-April. The first leg of the trade ends when the spread breaks lower a month later. After a quick corrective rally, resumption of the spread's advance signals a second phase of the short trade. That trade ends in early July with a rally in laggards, coupled with a sharp decline in the spread.

Both group and stock universes provide useful indications of momentum. Nonetheless, there are advantages to using group averages rather than individual stocks. Industry averages tend to cancel out stock-specific noise and therefore represent group themes more faithfully. And, as a practical matter, since a single group average is proxy for a larger number of individual issues, use of group indexes facilitates computation by reducing data load.

Notes

1. Victor Niederhoffer, *The Education of a Speculator* (New York: John Wiley & Sons, 1997).
2. Peter Brandt, *Diary of a Professional Commodity Trader* (Hoboken, NJ: John Wiley & Sons, 2011).

3. Jack D. Schwager, *Market Wizards* (New York: New York Institute of Finance, 1989).

4. This observation is consistent with the findings of other investigators. Robert Levy found that "five percent relative strength selection produced even better results than did ten percent selection." Robert A. Levy, *The Relative Strength Concept of Common Stock Price Forecasting* (New Rochelle, NY: Investors Intelligence, Inc., 1968).

5. The superior forward performance of relative-strength laggards is due to persistent contrarian bidding for "values" among laggard groups and stocks. We will examine that phenomenon more closely in Chapter 7.

6. Other studies confirm that forward performance is a function of relative strength. See: Robert A. Levy, "Relative Strength as a Criterion for Investment Selection," *Journal of Finance* 22 (December 1967); and Narasimhan Jegadeesh and Sheridan Titman, "Returns to Buying Winners and Selling Losers: Implications for Stock Market Efficiency," *Journal of Finance* 48 (March 1993).

7. Tobias J. Moskowitz and Mark Grinblatt, "Do Industries Explain Momentum?" *The Journal of Finance* 54, no. 4 (1999), www-stat.wharton.upenn.edu/~steele/Courses/956/Resource/Momentum/MoskowitzGrinblatt99.pdf.

CHAPTER 6

Why Jesse Went Broke

Alice started to her feet, for it flashed across her mind that she had never before seen a rabbit with either a waistcoat-pocket, or a watch to take out of it, and burning with curiosity, she ran across the field after it, and was just in time to see it pop down a large rabbit-hole under the hedge. In another moment down went Alice after it, never once considering how in the world she was to get out again.

—Lewis Carroll, *Alice's Adventures in Wonderland*[1]

Jesse Livermore discovered his knack for numbers in school, but when he reached 14, his father declared that Jesse could read and write passably well. Another pair of hands was needed full-time to clear the family's stone farm near South Acton, Massachusetts, and, literally, scratch a living from the thin soil. Within a few weeks Jesse resolved to leave the farm and make it on his own, and with $5 in his pocket and the blessing of his mother, he hitched a ride aboard a passing wagon and set out for Boston. Thus began the career of one of the most storied traders on Wall Street.

The wagon stopped on a busy street downtown, in front of the brokerage offices of Paine Webber. Sometimes the rabbit-hole is marked "Help Wanted."

> I got a job as quotation-board boy in a stock-brokerage office. I was quick at figures. At school I did three years of arithmetic in one. I was particularly good at mental arithmetic. As quotation-board boy I posted the numbers on the big board in the customers' room. One of the customers usually sat by the ticker and called out the prices. They couldn't come too fast for me. I have always remembered figures. No trouble at all.[2]

In the summer of 1892, Jesse turned 15. For six months he had recorded each tick of the stocks he was assigned. In his fertile mind patterns began to emerge.

> Those quotations did not represent prices of stocks to me, so many dollars per share. They were numbers. Of course, they meant something. They were always changing. It was all I had to be interested in—the changes. Why did they change? I didn't know. I didn't care. I didn't think about that. I simply saw that they changed. That was all I had to think about five hours every day and two on Saturdays: that they were always changing.[3]

Jesse kept a "dope book," jotting down prices, looking for "parallelisms of behavior." That summer, another young quotation-board boy approached Jesse. He had heard a rumor that could send Burlington shares higher, and he needed a partner to meet the margin required by a local bucket shop. Jesse checked his dope book.

> Sure enough, Burlington, according to my figuring, was acting as it usually did before it went up. I had never gambled with the other boys. But all I could see was that this was a grand chance to test the accuracy of my work, of my hobby. It struck me at once that if my dope didn't work in practice there was nothing in the theory of it to interest anybody. So I gave him all I had, and with our pooled resources he went to one of the near-by bucket shops and bought some Burlington. Two days later we cashed in. I made a profit of $3.12.[4]

Livermore began trading at the bucket shops on his own, basing trades on the patterns he discerned in his dope book. Before long, he was making enough money to devote his full time to trading. Within a year, he had accumulated over $1,000, equivalent to about $25,000 today.

Jesse was a trend follower, not a contrarian. "I never buy on reactions or go short on rallies," he wrote later. "My theory is that behind . . . major movements is an irresistible force. Just recognize that the movement is there and take advantage of it by steering your speculative ship along with the tide."[5] Livermore was committed to following what he called "the line of least resistance."

By 1906, at 29, Jesse had been trading professionally for nearly 15 years and had accumulated enough capital to assume positions totaling half a million. In the spring of that year he began to build short positions. Then, on

April 18, 1906, the San Francisco earthquake struck. The market up to that point had been bullish, and on the day following the quake, stocks dropped only a little, barely registering the effects of what would ultimately prove to be a catastrophe. By the third day, however, news of the full impact of the quake reached Wall Street, and the market tumbled. Livermore booked a profit of $300,000 (See Figure 6.1).

Call money began to dry up during the decline, and rates rose, forcing traders to scramble for capital to protect their margined long positions. Livermore became convinced that the market would decline further, so he began to build a new short position as 1906 drew to a close. Stocks continued to weaken, and by early 1907 his trades showed substantial profits. He closed out his positions and left for a well-earned vacation in Europe.

While in Paris, Livermore read in the *Paris Herald* that Smelters Corporation had rallied on news of a dividend increase.

> I knew that all bull manipulation was foredoomed to failure in that bear market. The instant I read the dispatch I knew there was only one thing to do to be comfortable, and that was to sell Smelters short. Why, the insiders as much as begged me on their knees to do it, when they increased the dividend rate on the verge of a money panic.[6]

FIGURE 6.1 Dow Jones Industrial Average

Jesse returned to New York immediately and began to sell short in earnest. On October 24, 1907, panic struck.

> Reports from the money crowd early indicated that borrowers would have to pay whatever the lenders saw fit to ask. There wouldn't be enough to go around. That day the money crowd was much larger than usual. When delivery time came that afternoon there must have been a hundred brokers around the Money Post, each hoping to borrow the money that his firm urgently needed. Without money they must sell what stocks they were carrying on margin—sell at any price they could get in a market where buyers were as scarce as money—and just when there was not a dollar in sight.[7]

Near the end of the trading session, a representative of J.P. Morgan strode to the Money Post and announced a $10 million line of credit. Morgan had halted the decline, but Livermore knew that the market was still vulnerable and contemplated adding substantially to his short positions on the next day. That afternoon, a mutual friend of Morgan and Livermore approached Jesse. Morgan requested that Livermore not only close his short positions but start buying. Jesse began covering immediately and continued his buying on the next day's open.

Livermore's one-day profit at the end of trading on October 24 exceeded $1 million. Perhaps of even more significance to Jesse, J.P. Morgan had personally acknowledged Livermore's success and influence. "He was a man, J.P. Morgan was. They don't come much bigger. . . . That is why I said to my friends that my dream had come true and that I had been king for a moment. . . . It was a day of days for me."[8]

Seven years later, Jesse was broke.

The Cotton King

After a string of spectacular successes, Livermore entered a cotton trade based, not on his own trend-following system, but on the advice of a brilliant cotton trader, Percy Thomas, known on Wall Street as the Cotton King. The two met in Palm Beach, a favorite vacation spot of Jesse's, and became friends. Over time, the articulate and erudite cotton trader convinced Livermore to join him in a long trade based on crop information Thomas had received through his network of agents. Thomas was convincing, and despite Livermore's initially bearish observations, he agreed to join Thomas.

Cotton started to decline. Instead of taking a quick loss, Livermore attempted to support the market by buying more.

> It was the most asinine play of my career. . . . The market didn't act the way it should have acted had Thomas been right. Having taken the first wrong step I took the second and the third . . . I allowed myself to be persuaded not only into not taking my loss but into holding up the market. That is a style of play foreign to my nature and contrary to my trading principles and theories. Even as a boy in the bucket shops I had known better. But I was not myself. I was another man—a Thomasized person.[9]

Livermore lost nearly all the profit he had made during the 1906 bear market. Still, he had a considerable stake of $300,000. But now Jesse needed $200,000 to meet an "urgent" expense. Rather than expend his remaining capital, he tried to force the market to give him what he needed in trading profits. Another lesson learned the hard way: "The hope of making the stock market pay your bills is one of the most prolific sources of loss in Wall Street."[10]

Livermore approached the new decade a wiser but poorer man. He was resolved to avoid the costly mistakes of the last few years by single-mindedly following his own price-based system. His problem now was the market itself.

1911–1914

> "Well, in our country," said Alice, still panting a little, "you'd generally get to somewhere else if you ran very fast for a long time, as we've been doing."
> "A slow sort of country!" said the Queen. "Now, here, you see, it takes all the running you can do to keep in the same place."
>
> —*Lewis Carroll*[11]

The years from 1911 to 1914 were eventful, not only in the United States but worldwide. In the fall of 1911, the Norwegian explorer Roald Amundsen reached the South Pole. The next year, the Titanic hit an iceberg and

Woodrow Wilson won the U.S. presidency in a three-way race. In 1913 the 16th Amendment to the U.S. Constitution authorized the federal income tax, while the 17th mandated the popular election of senators. A treaty ending the First Balkan War was signed in May of that year, and by June the Second Balkan War had begun. Charlie Chaplin debuted in the film comedy *Making a Living* in February 1914. Four months later, Archduke Ferdinand of Austria and his wife were assassinated. That summer Babe Ruth made his first major league appearance with the Red Sox as Europe mobilized for war.

After years of extended trends in both directions, prices on the New York Stock Exchange settled into a range. For a trend follower like Livermore, truncated trends and frequent reversals made trading difficult, if not treacherous (Figure 6.2 shows the Dow Jones Industrial Average from 1911 to 1914).

> The market flattened out. Things drifted from bad to worse. I not only lost all I had but got into debt again—more heavily than ever. Those were long lean years, 1911, 1912, 1913 and 1914. There was no money to be made. The opportunity simply wasn't there and so I was worse off than ever.[12]

Livermore took away a lesson from this period, which he later formulated into a rule:

FIGURE 6.2 Dow Jones Industrial Average 1911–1914

This experience has been the experience of so many traders so many times that I can give this rule: In a narrow market, when prices are not getting anywhere to speak of but move within a narrow range, there is no sense in trying to anticipate what the next big movement is going to be—up or down.[13]

Livermore's observation makes a good deal of sense, but how is the rule to be followed? How could Livermore have known that the market would narrow? The adversity he encountered this time was not of his own making. He followed his trading rules. They just didn't work.

The performance spread offers insight into Livermore's difficulties. In the following study, monthly data and a seven-month look-back are used to compute the relative strength of 75 stocks from that period.[14] In Figure 6.3, the running one-month forward performance of the strongest and weakest 8 percent of those stocks is shown.

FIGURE 6.3 Forward Performance of RS Leaders and Laggards

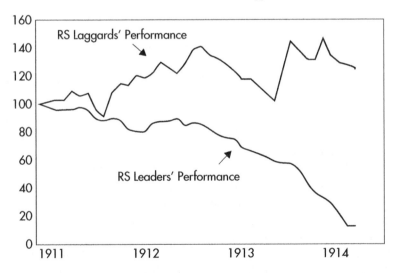

From 1911 to mid-1914, the forward performance of RS leaders was consistently negative. Any trend follower taking long positions in strong stocks would have done poorly. Shorts in the weakest stocks would not have fared better, since those issues managed a net gain. Because the dominant dynamic during this period was negative feedback, the broad list meandered within a range as traders sold into strength and bought into weakness.

FIGURE 6.4 Performance Spread

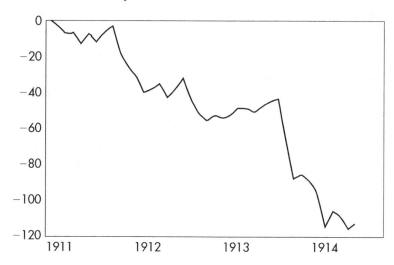

The performance spread fell persistently from the beginning of 1911 (see Figure 6.4).

Negative feedback is hazardous for trend followers, and even close risk control may not save the hapless trader from substantial losses. Had Jesse the means to compute the performance spread, he would no doubt have recognized early on that conditions did not favor his trend-following approach and perhaps ceased trading in time to preserve his remaining capital. His experience illustrates that during periods of negative feedback, when contrarians are dominant, a simple trend-following strategy does not work.

In June 1914, when Archduke Ferdinand was assassinated, rumors of war began to spread. In July, Austria-Hungary declared war on Serbia, and in that same month Germany declared war on Russia. Most foreign stock exchanges were already closed when, in July 1914, the New York Stock Exchange shut down operations. But not before prices broke sharply in the final month of trading (see Figure 6.5).

During that last month of trading, laggard stocks were hit hardest as the broad market fell (see Figure 6.6).

As the advance in the performance spread shows, the July decline was driven by positive feedback (see Figure 6.7). This was a strong, albeit short-lived, momentum-driven trend of the sort supportive of Jesse's trend-following

FIGURE 6.5   Dow Jones Industrial Average

FIGURE 6.6   Forward Performance of RS Leaders and Laggards

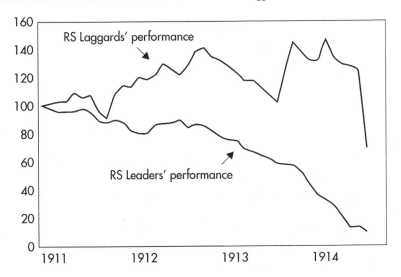

FIGURE 6.7   Performance Spread

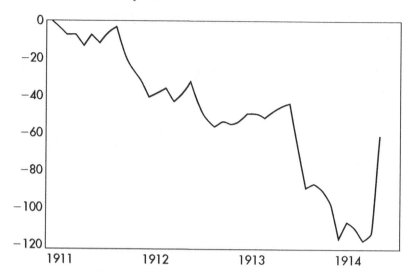

strategy. But it was too late. Both Jesse and his capital were exhausted. Now in debt well over $1 million, Livermore was forced to declare bankruptcy.

The Final Years

> "But that's just the trouble with me," said Alice. "I give myself very good advice, but I very seldom follow it."
>
> —*Lewis Carroll*[15]

Jesse's fortunes improved during strongly trending bull and bear markets that followed, and when Livermore closed out his short positions after the Crash of 1929, he was reputedly worth well over $100 million. The 1930s, however, experienced a significant degree of mean reversion.[16] Not much is known of Livermore's trading during those years, but his trend-following approach failed him again. This was a period driven by negative feedback and dominated by risk-averse, contrarian traders. During those years, there were five separate months during which a trend-following strategy would have lost over 40 percent. Each instance came as the market rose substantially.[17] In

1934, Jesse was again forced to declare bankruptcy, and on March 7 of that year, he was suspended as a member of the Chicago Board of Trade.

"Tut, tut, child!" said the Duchess. "Everything's got a moral, if only you can find it."

—*Lewis Carroll*[18]

Jesse Livermore's story is a cautionary tale for any trader, but above all for trend followers. There is a natural tendency to see locally successful solutions as global solutions, and perhaps Jesse fell into that error, one that led him resolutely to pursue a single method through varying conditions. We have seen that the market alternates between two opposed dynamics and that, as a result, no approach to trading works all the time. If there is a moral to be gained from Jesse's story, it is that trend following can be very profitable when it is working, but can also prove disastrous when it is not. Unfortunately for Jesse, he had no way to determine when his methods were likely to work and when they were not. Fortunately for us, we have the spread.

Notes

1. Lewis Carroll, *Alice's Adventures in Wonderland*, Chapter One: "Down the Rabbit Hole" (London: Macmillan and Co., 1865).
2. Edwin Lefevre, *Reminiscences of a Stock Operator* (New York: George H. Doran Company, 1923).
3. Ibid.
4. Ibid.
5. Jesse Livermore, *How to Trade in Stocks* (New York: Duell, Sloan and Pearce, 1940).
6. Lefevre, *Reminiscences*.
7. Ibid.
8. Ibid.
9. Ibid.
10. Ibid.
11. Lewis Carroll, *Through the Looking-Glass and What Alice Found There* (London: Macmillan and Co., 1871).
12. Lefevre, *Reminiscences*.

13. Ibid.

14. Historical data provided by Yale School of Management, International Center for Finance.

15. Carroll, *Alice's Adventures in Wonderland.*

16. Narasimhan Jegadeesh and Sheridan Titman, "Returns to Buying Winners and Selling Losers: Implications for Stock Market Efficiency," *Journal of Finance* 48 (March 1993).

17. Ibid.

18. Carroll, *Alice's Adventures in Wonderland.*

CHAPTER 7

Sheep Dogs and Other Contrarians

> *I sometimes think that speculation must be an unnatural sort of business,*
> *because I find that the average speculator has arrayed against him his*
> *own nature.*
>
> —Jesse Livermore, *How to Trade in Stocks*[1]

People began lining up in the rain hours before Target's Buffalo store opened for business on Black Friday 2010. At 4:00 A.M., manager Ben Gregory unlocked the doors, and a torrent of shoppers poured in. Keith Krantz, who had been waiting eight hours for a chance to buy a sale-priced flat-screen TV, was pinned against the metal door frame in the surge, then shoved to the ground. He screamed in pain as shoppers stepped over, around, and on him in their frenzy to snatch up bargains. Keith thought at that moment he might die. He told an interviewer at the hospital, "I was thinking I don't want to die here on the ground. That's exactly what I thought." Keith was lucky. Exactly two years earlier, 34-year-old WalMart employee Jdimytai Damour was trampled to death by shoppers when the doors of the Valley Stream store in Long Island opened on Black Friday.

While the behavior of bargain hunters is at times deplorable, the attractiveness of a bargain is self-evident. We all understand immediately what drives bargain hunting. The impulse is built in, an integral part of a larger scheme of dispositions which shapes our everyday behavior. So powerful is this fragment of our own nature that most of us carry the habit into our trading.

If a man is offered a fact which goes against his instincts, he will scrutinize it closely, and unless the evidence is overwhelming, he will refuse to believe it. If, on the other hand, he is offered something which affords a reason for acting in accordance to his instincts, he will accept it even on the slightest evidence.

—*Bertrand Russell*[2]

We are by nature contrarian, so it is only natural to seek support in narratives that accord with our instinctive sense of how things work. Most new traders assume that profits are won by first detecting bargains overlooked by others and then selling once the real value of the asset is broadly realized. Even practiced contrarian traders fancy that they lean against the crowd, against the majority. But do they? As William Eckhardt observes in Jack D. Schwager's *New Market Wizards*, "if you bring normal human habits and tendencies to trading, you'll gravitate toward the majority." If Eckhardt is right, then contrarians make up the majority of traders. Eckhardt adds, "In the long run, the majority loses."[3]

If so, there is something heroic in contrarians' stand against the odds. Perhaps for that reason, contrarian victories, when they come, are that much sweeter and make for memorable stories. When asked about their best experiences by the authors of *Traders*, most interviewees spoke of making a great deal of money or of taking a large position.

However, several responded to this open-ended question by talking in explicitly contrarian terms; the best trade was seen as the one which proved their theory right in the face of arguments to the contrary, irrespective of profitability.[4]

Trades of any stripe may prove profitable, and some who choose contrarian trade-entry methods have done extremely well, including Warren Buffet, David Dreman,[5] John Neff,[6] and Jim Rogers. These traders are not just among the contrarian majority but also among a minority of successful traders. Successful contrarians tend to be value investors who invest over the long term, a strategy supported by academic investigation.[7] In this chapter, we will examine the dynamics of contrarian trading, including opportunities as well as threats present during contrarian-dominated episodes.

The Sheep Dog Effect

Both the stock and group universes we've examined so far include selections from a diversified list of industries. But what happens to feedback dynamics when a universe is not diversified? In the next study, 151 bank stocks make up a single-industry universe for analysis.[8] Figure 7.1 sums the average daily changes of those bank stocks from February 1997 through early June 2011.

Figure 7.2 shows the running sum of forward changes in the strongest and weakest 10 percent of the bank stock universe. Note that the forward performance of relative strength (RS) leaders trends lower while that of RS laggards advances.

As a consequence of the negative divergence of bank stock leaders and laggards, the performance spread between the top and bottom 10 percent of the universe declines steadily and confirms a dynamic of chronic negative feedback (see Figure 7.3).

Because exogenous economic factors that affect one bank usually affect all banks to some degree, traders naturally expect stocks within the group to move together. So when one stock trades out of line with others, traders note the anomaly and respond in a way that repairs the discrepancy. The

FIGURE 7.1 Bank Stock Average (Log Scale)

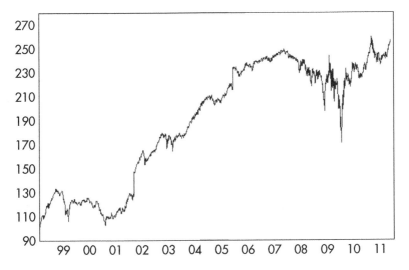

FIGURE 7.2   Forward Performance of Bank Stock Leaders and Laggards

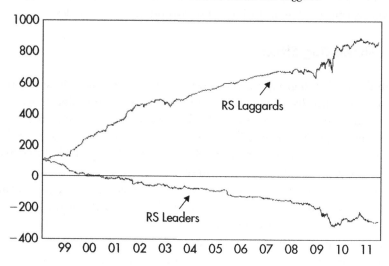

FIGURE 7.3   Bank Stock Performance Spread

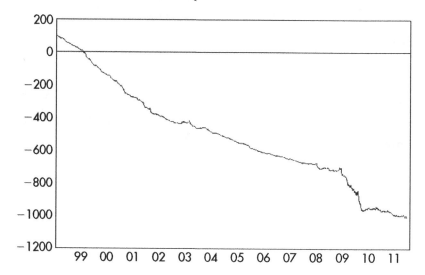

performance spread constantly declines because negative-feedback traders persist in turning outliers near both perimeters of the universe back toward the benchmark equivalence line (BEL). Stocks that are significantly stronger than the group average are viewed as overpriced and are offered, while laggards receive a bid. In effect, traders act like sheep dogs, chasing stocks that stray too far afield back into the fold. Generalizing, any universe of thematically related stocks tends to huddle like a herd of sheep under the watchful eyes of contrarian shepherds. It follows that a universe of stocks is likely to exhibit a rising spread only if selections are thematically diversified.

A Contrarian Hedge?

Since bank stock leaders and laggards are negatively correlated, does a hedged trade, short of leaders and long of laggards, generate sustained profits? Notional long profits from the laggard 10 percent of bank stocks averaged an impressive 0.22 percent daily, twice the 0.11 percent daily profit from shorts in the strongest bank stocks. Skewed results favoring laggard longs are consistent with the bullish trend of the average bank stock over most of the period.

Hedged strategies utilizing the top and bottom 5, 10, and 20 percent of the bank stock universe all showed profits before any allowance for trading costs. Average daily change and portfolio turnover for each are shown below (Table 7.1).[9]

Portfolio turnover in each category is high. Weak stocks that rally well quickly lose their laggard status and are replaced by other stocks that qualify as laggard, while shorts in the strongest stocks are exited once those stocks fall from leadership. Because leaders and laggards change rapidly under negative

TABLE 7.1 Results of Hedged Strategies

Series	Average Daily Change	Average Daily Turnover
5% Leaders	−.11%	50%
5% Laggards	+.23%	70%
10% Leaders	−.11%	41%
10% Laggards	+.22%	42%
20% Leaders	−.09%	31%
20% Laggards	+.18%	32%

feedback, to execute the proposed contrarian hedge, multiple trades must be made as often as daily.[10] Costs of execution, including commissions and slippage, would likely erode posted results considerably. However, the persistence of negative feedback is prima facie evidence that artful contrarians have found a way to profit from the trade. More generally, if contrarians could not find profitable opportunities, there would be few contrarians, and without contrarians, the dialectic that sustains the market would collapse.

The Contrarian Rebound

It is always the same. At some point during a momentum-driven decline, a switch flips in the collective mind of traders. They become skeptical enough of the extended move that they turn contrarian and fade the trend. Contrarian traders are net buyers at such times because there are oversold bargains at hand, but they are not bullish. They have little confidence that rallies will be sustained, and they are prepared to take profits on a rebound.

The territory around bear market lows is prime hunting ground for contrarians seeking bargains. The weakest, most oversold stocks then receive the strongest bids and, as a result, recover faster than stocks that held up relatively well during the preceding decline. This contrarian phenomenon is reliable enough to be counted upon. The initial phase of a bull market *always* begins as a correction, driven by negative feedback and signaled by a falling performance spread.

The historically strongest stocks are not likely to be the best selections near the bottom of a bear market. . . . The continuation of relative strength concept produces superior results during all periods except those immediately succeeding a comparatively weak market.

—*Robert A. Levy*[11]

Since, in our lexicon, a bear market is a momentum-driven decline, we may recast Levy's formulation more positively:

The historically weakest stocks are likely to be the best (long) selections after a momentum-driven decline.

Just as an archer generates and stores energy by drawing a bow, positive feedback during a bear market pulls leaders and laggards apart, generating and storing energy as structural difference. The ensuing corrective rally is propelled by the energy released when RS differences collapse.

Toward the end of a bear market rally, the RS gap between leaders and laggards has narrowed. Energy stored during the previous decline has been spent, and contrarian bids fall off. The initial, corrective phase is over, and the market is now at a tipping point. Just when a bear market rally appears close to exhaustion, the switch in traders' heads may unaccountably flip again, this time the other way. No longer skeptical and risk averse, they exhibit new confidence in the immediate direction of price. Instead of hunting for bargains among laggard issues, they turn the focus of their buying to groups and stocks leading the rally higher. Not all bear market corrections morph into bull markets, but when they do, a rising spread signals the transition from contrarian rebound to a new, momentum-driven phase.

In the examples of bear market corrections offered below, the forward performance of RS leaders and laggards, as well as the performance spread, are shown. In each case, the performance spread falls during the initial phase of recovery as RS laggards outpace RS leaders to the upside.

In the spring of 1998, a momentum-driven decline began which cut 50 percent from the price of laggard groups by that fall (Figure 7.4). The first, contrarian phase of the rally began in September but lasted just two months, after which a rising performance spread announced resumption of the secular bull market.

FIGURE 7.4   May 1998—February 1999

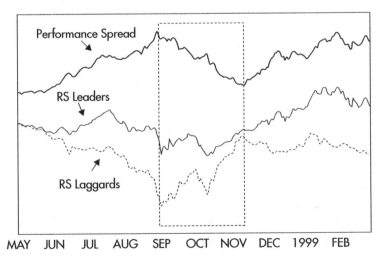

FIGURE 7.5 May 2002—September 2003

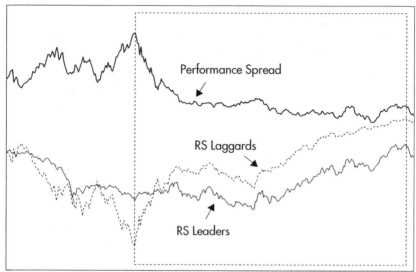

MAY JUN JUL AUG SEP OCT NOV DEC 2003 FEB MAR APR MAY JUN JUL AUG SEP

In April of 2000, the S&P 500 topped 1,500, but by October of 2002, the most severe bear market since the 1970s had cut the price of the index in half. The rebound from the October low was typical, as energetic RS laggards outran lethargic RS leaders to the upside (see Figure 7.5). A retest sent prices moderately lower, but a flat spread indicated weak downside momentum. Then in March of 2003, a second contrarian-sponsored rally took both leaders and laggards higher. The spread fell only slightly during this rally, evidence that most of the energy generated and stored during the bear market had been exhausted in the October to December contrarian rally.

Following the "flash crash" of 2008, RS laggards were conspicuous beneficiaries of contrarian bargain hunting during the rebound following the March 2009 low (see Figure 7.6).

The contrarian rebound is a regular feature after bear market bottoms, but not all contrarian rallies mark the beginning of a new bull market. Contrarian rallies are, by our definition, corrective, and any number of corrections may interrupt an extended bear market. As our examples demonstrate, until confirmed by a rising spread, the initial, contrarian-driven phase of a bull market is indistinguishable from a bear market correction.

A broad decline began in 2000, and in action definitive of momentum-driven declines, laggards outpaced RS leaders to the downside (see Figure 7.7).

FIGURE 7.6 August 2008—August 2009

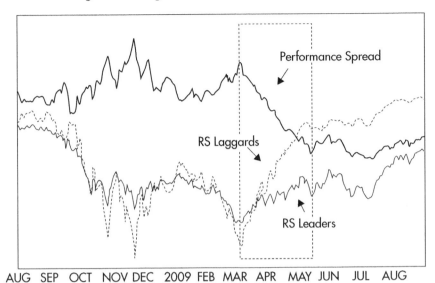

AUG SEP OCT NOV DEC 2009 FEB MAR APR MAY JUN JUL AUG

FIGURE 7.7 May 2001—June 2002

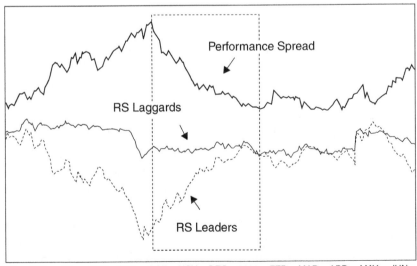

MAY JUN JUL AUG SEP OCT NOV DEC 2002 FEB MAR APR MAY JUN

A rebound from fall 2001 lows featured RS laggards, and the performance spread fell as the market rose. The rally during that fall and winter was identical in every respect to corrective recoveries that initiate bull markets. In early 2002 the spread rose a bit before stalling as group leaders and laggards meandered through the next three months. In April the spread began to rise, but the transition to a rising spread did not mark the beginning of a new bull market. Instead, momentum pointed the way lower, and the bear market resumed.

The Contrarian Collapse

A market can and does often cease to be a bull market long before prices generally begin to break. My long expected warning came to me when I noticed that one after another, those stocks which had been the leaders of the market reacted several points from the top and—for the first time in many months—did not come back.

—*Jesse Livermore*[12]

This proposition is a familiar one to market traders. The stocks which are strongest just prior to a bear market are often those that suffer a substantial price decline when the bear market begins.

—*Robert A. Levy*[13]

Contrarian herding is seen not only near bear market bottoms, but as well around bull market tops, though not with the same dependable regularity. Once a bull market has peaked, traders sometimes take profits in RS leaders earlier and more decisively than in laggard issues. Laggards may even improve as bids shift from stronger to weaker stocks. The behavior of RS leaders during the spring of 2000 is a good example of the contrarian collapse (see Figure 7.8). A powerful bull market had lifted favored stocks, mostly technology and Internet issues, to large premiums over laggards. Once traders began to take profits, inflated RS leaders fell sharply. The decline in leaders gave laggards a boost as traders, still bullish but now less inclined to take on risk, retreated into dependable blue chips, which had lagged during the advance.

A normal bull market correction is a pause within a longer uptrend. Prices react then recover to new highs. A contrarian collapse, on the other hand, is a deathblow to a bull market. It is a correction from which there is no recovery. The difference between a normal correction and a contrarian collapse is one of

FIGURE 7.8 Contrarian Collapse—Spring 2000

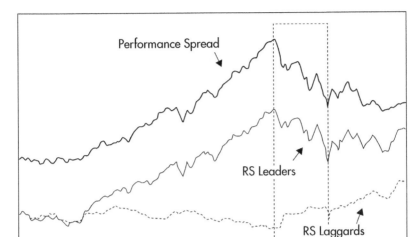

degree, not kind. I know of no way definitively to distinguish a contrarian collapse from other bull market corrections, but note that historically such reversals have occurred only after sustained, momentum-driven advances.

A contrarian collapse knocks strong groups out of market leadership and often into the bottom quartile of RS. It is not unusual for strong groups to drop collectively by 20 percent or more within several months. The contrarian collapse, like the contrarian rebound, is corrective. Since all corrections are countertrend moves, trading these episodes is risky business. However, given the long-term bullish bias of traders, attempting to profit by shorting RS leaders during a contrarian collapse is particularly hazardous.

Black Monday

On October 19, 1987, the Dow Jones Industrial average declined 22.6 percent in the largest single-day drop in history. The decline on Black Monday was nearly twice that of Black Tuesday on October 29, 1929. From the opening of the market on October 14, 1987, through the close on October 19, the major U.S. stock indexes fell on average more than 30 percent. Academics have been scratching their heads since trying to account for the suddenness and severity of the decline. Computer trading, the use of derivatives, illiquidity generated by massive sell orders, less-restrictive margin requirements, and overvaluation have all been offered as explanations. Our concern is not with such accounts, but with traders' behavior. Specifically, would the indicators developed so far have offered practical aid to momentum traders?

The opening bell on January 2, 1987, began a rally that added more than 40 percent to the Dow Jones 30 by late August (see Figure 7.9). A normal-looking correction from the August high shaved a little more than 8 percent from the index before prices rallied again into the early days of October. The index gave little indication of what was to follow.

FIGURE 7.9   Dow Jones Industrial Average—1987

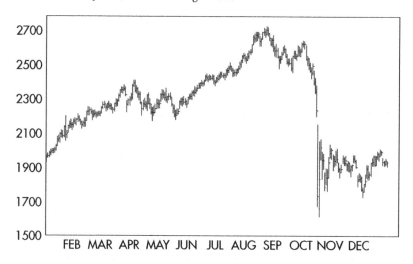

The forward performances of RS leaders and laggards tell another story.[14] Through early May, momentum advanced leaders faster than laggards, but then leaders began to flag as laggards outran leaders to the upside (see Figure 7.10). On the evidence, traders had become less inclined to pursue the strongest stocks and now preferred other issues that had lagged during the previous advance. This behavior suggests that traders were turning risk averse and contrarian, even as the market continued to rally.

These indications are confirmed by the performance spread, which rose during the first four months of the year before peaking in May (see Figure 7.11). The decline in the performance spread from that point was punctuated by rallies in July and September, neither of which threatened the overall declining trend of the series. The failure of momentum signaled by the irregular descent of the

FIGURE 7.10 Stock Leaders and Laggards—1987

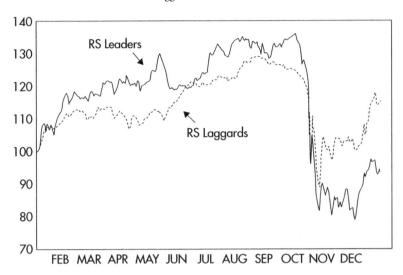

FIGURE 7.11 Performance Spread—1987

performance spread after May issued a clear warning that the summer rally was losing momentum.

The relative strength spread gave indications of a loss of momentum similar to those offered by the performance spread (see Figure 7.12).

FIGURE 7.12   Relative Strength Spread—1987

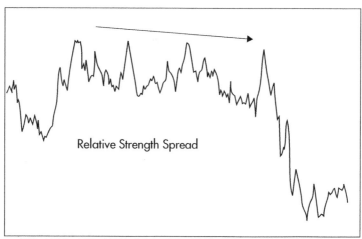

FEB MAR APR MAY JUN JUL AUG SEP OCT NOV DEC

By late August, declines in both versions of the spread confirmed the absence of positive feedback. The subsequent price decline that October was attended by falling spreads, evidence that the drop was not a momentum-driven bear market, but a deep correction within a longer-term bull market.

Notes

1. Jesse Livermore, *How to Trade in Stocks* (New York: Duell, Sloan and Pearce, 1940).
2. Bertrand Russell, *The Will to Doubt* (New York: Philosophical Library, 1958).
3. Jack D. Schwager, *The New Market Wizards* (New York: Harper Collins, 1992).
4. Mark Fenton-O'Creevy, Nigel Nicholson, Emma Soane, and Paul Willman, *Traders: Risks, Decisions, and Management in Financial Markets* (New York: Oxford University Press, 2005).

5. Chairman of Dreman Value Management.
6. Head of Vanguard's Windsor Fund from 1964 to 1995.
7. Eugene F. Fama and Kenneth R. French, "The Cross-Section of Expected Stock Returns," *Journal of Finance* 47, no. 2 (1992); and Josef Lakonishok, Andrei Shleifer and Robert W. Vishny, "Contrarian Investment, Extrapolation, and Risk," *Journal of Finance* 49, no. 5 (1994).
8. Some of the 151 bank stocks in this study are thinly traded, and as a practical matter would be difficult to trade actively:

ABCB	BOKF	CHCO	FFIN	FWV	LARK	NPBC	RF	STI	UMBF
AIB	BPFH	CHFC	FFKT	GABC	LION	NRIM	RNST	STL	UNTY
AROW	BTFG	CMA	FFKY	GBCI	MBFI	NTRS	RY	STT	USB
ASBC	BXS	CNAF	FHN	GFED	MBVT	OFG	SAN	SUBK	UVSP
ASRV	C	CNBKA	FITB	GSBC	METR	OKSB	SASR	SUSQ	VIST
AUBN	CACB	CPF	FLIC	HARL	MFLR	ONB	SAVB	SYBT	VLY
BAC	CATY	CTBI	FMBI	HBAN	MI	PCBC	SBCF	TCB	WABC
BANF	CBIN	CVBF	FMER	HBHC	MSFG	PEBK	SBIB	TCBK	WASH
BAP	CBSH	CYN	FMFC	HEOP	MSL	PEBO	SCBT	THFF	WBK
BBT	CBU	ESBK	FNB	HIFS	MTB	PNBC	SFNC	TMP	WBS
BCS	CCBG	FBMI	FRBK	IBCP	MTU	PNBK	SIVB	TRMK	WCBOD
BKSC	CEBK	FBNC	FRME	IBKC	NBBC	PNC	SRCE	TRST	WFC
BLX	CFFC	FCF	FSBI	INDB	NBN	PRK	STBA	UBCP	WSBC
BMO	CFNB	FCNCA	FULT	JPM	NBTB	QCRH	STBC	UBSH	WSFS
BOH	CFR	FFBC	FUNC	KEY	NBTF	RBPAA	STD	UBSI	WTNY
									ZION

9. The back test assumes that dollar amounts short and long are equalized daily.
10. During periods of positive feedback, the lists of leaders and laggards do not change as rapidly, since under those conditions strong stocks tend to remain strong, and weak stocks, weak.
11. Robert A. Levy, *The Relative Strength Concept of Common Stock Price Forecasting* (New York: Investors Intelligence, Inc., 1968).
12. Livermore, *How to Trade in Stocks.*

13. Levy, *The Relative Strength Concept of Common Stock Price Formatting*.
14. These 151 stocks make up the universe used in this analysis:

AA	BEAM	CSX	FRT	IBM	LIZ	NEE	PH	SON	UIS
AAPL	BP	CVS	FTR	IDCC	LLY	NEM	PL	SVU	UNP
AEP	BRS	DBD	GCI	IDTI	LNC	NEU	PNR	SWK	UNT
AET	CAG	DDS	GFI	IFF	LNT	NFG	PRX	SWKS	USB
AIG	CANE	DE	GMT	IP	LPX	NOC	PSA	T	UTX
ALK	CAT	DNB	GPC	IR	MAS	NYT	PVH	TAOM	UVV
AMD	CBE	DOV	GR	IRF	MAT	OKE	R	TAP	VFC
ASH	CDE	DOW	GT	JCP	MCD	OLN	ROK	TDW	VMC
ATO	CFR	DPL	HAL	JPM	MDR	OMX	RPM	TGT	VZ
AVP	CI	DUK	HAS	K	MGA	OSG	RRD	THC	WHR
AVY	CINF	EMR	HL	KEY	MHP	OXY	RSH	TKR	WMB
AXP	CL	ESL	HNZ	KGC	MMM	PBI	RYL	TM	WPO
BA	CLX	F	HPQ	KLAC	MOLX	PCH	SLB	TMK	WY
BAC	COP	FDX	HSC	KMT	MUR	PEG	SNA	TXI	XOM
BAX	CP	FLS	HSY	KO	NBL	PG	SNE	TXT	XRX
									ZION

CHAPTER 8

Situational Awareness

The pilot received two weather briefings and was advised of deteriorating weather in the destination area. When he filed an instrument flight plan en route, he told the briefer that he did not have his approach plates on board. Radar data disclosed that the aircraft flew the approach at least 1,000 feet too high and at a higher than normal speed for the approach. Air Traffic Control instructed the pilot to immediately execute a missed approach. The pilot responded, "I guess I don't know where I am." Radar data then showed the aircraft climbing and descending rapidly, then descending to 300 feet above the ground as it neared the western airport boundary. Four seconds later, the aircraft impacted the departure end of the runway. Ground witnesses observed the aircraft narrowly miss a building, then turn sharply toward the runway before descending steeply to impact.

—From the National Transportation Safety Board
Report LAX97FA049

Situational awareness has been defined as "perception of the elements in the environment, the comprehension of their meaning and the projection of their status in the near future."[1] Or, to put it simply, knowing where you are. Gaining situational awareness requires a mental map, or model, of the territory and the information necessary to locate one's position on the map. The hapless pilot cited above had the requisite instrumentation in his panel, but missing was an approach plate, or a model of the territory.

During landings under instrument meteorological conditions, when visual cues are minimal, navigational instruments and approach plates provide situational awareness. Figure 8.1 shows an instrument approach plate for Brown Field in San Diego.

FIGURE 8.1 Approach Plate—San Diego/Brown Field

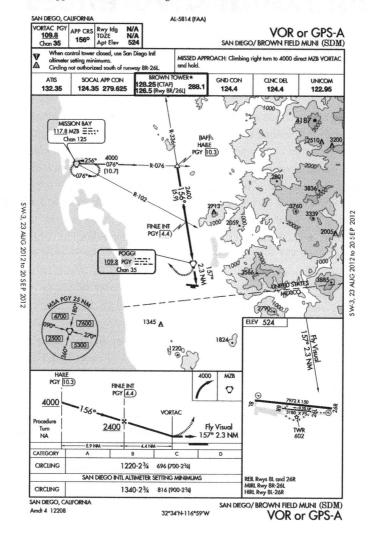

The approach plate offers a strategy for landing safely. Designed and published by the Federal Aeronautics Administration, strategies are tested for safety and efficiency, and all relevant conditions within the airport environment, including terrain and obstructions, are taken into account. Considerable planning and testing make it unnecessary for the pilot to reinvent a landing strategy on the fly. The pilot's job is to execute the approach using the plate and the instruments in his flight panel.

While an approach plate provides a fixed strategy, the conditions under which a pilot must fly may vary from flight to flight. Choices must be made, and the pilot has a reasonable amount of discretion. The first decision is always go/no-go. If cloud ceilings are below required minimums, or wind and weather make a successful landing unlikely, then the pilot may elect to remain on the ground until conditions improve or, if already in flight, to choose an alternate airport where landing risks are acceptable. Once the pilot commits to the approach, altitude, crosswinds, icing and thunderstorms may be factors for which a pilot must make adjustments. Safely executing an approach under instrument flight conditions requires considerable expertise. A combination of training and strategic clarity accounts for the relative safety of air travel.

Like a pilot, the trader must take in, analyze, and act on multiple inputs that change rapidly. However, traders' outcomes have been generally disastrous. Most traders lose money.[2] There are many reasons, but among them is likely the attempt to trade without a well-defined strategy.

Bielema's Choice

Old Scout: "Billy, you don't put a team together with a computer!"
Billy Beane: "Adapt or die."

—Moneyball

You are the coach. Your football team has a one-touchdown lead over a well-matched opponent in the first quarter of the title game. Your last three offensive plays have netted seven yards, and you now face a fourth down with three yards to go for a first on the opponent's 38-yard line. You have three options: Punt, attempt a field goal, or go for a first down. What is your decision? Perhaps you'd like to take a time out.

First-year coach of the Wisconsin Badgers, Bret Bielema, faced just this situation in the 2012 Rose Bowl. On the other side of the field, Chip Kelly, coach of the Oregon Ducks, knew exactly what he would do given these same conditions, but now he waited for Bielema's decision. He was not disappointed. Bielema chose to punt.

Economist David Romer offered a fresh look at strategic decision making in his study of data from over 700 National Football League (NFL) games, in which he calculated the expected points (EPs) for each of the three fourth-down options.[3] His analysis shows that Bielema's best choice statistically was to go for a first down. The Badgers could expect to net zero points by punting, while a first down under these conditions is expected to yield positive EP. A field goal was the least favorable option since, on average, a kick from that position on the field gives the opposition a slight point advantage.[4]

For the vast majority watching that game, Bielema's choice was not remarkable. Doubtless those of us who have gained a little football savvy over many seasons of coaching from the couch would also have elected to punt. We are in good company. Romer found that on 1,068 fourth-down situations, when going for it was the optimal choice, coaches instead elected to punt 959 times.

Bielema followed his gut, and his decision appeared justified when Wisconsin's punt backed Oregon up against its own goal line. But he did not take into account Oregon's explosive offense. On second down, with three seconds remaining in the quarter, De'Anthony Thomas ran a right sweep for 91 yards and a touchdown. Oregon went on to win the Rose Bowl by seven points.

Brian Burke, a former U.S. Navy carrier pilot with a BS in aerospace engineering, followed his geeky passion for football by analyzing 2,400 NFL games played from 2000 to 2008. Burke used data from only the first and third quarters to avoid anomalies resulting from hurried decisions or desperate calls late in a half. He calculated the expected points from a first down at various distances from the goal then smoothed the data to generate estimates of EP at every distance from the end zone (see Figure 8.2).

Burke calculated the EP indifference curve between fourth-down options given two variables, yards from a touchdown and yards to go for a first down (see Figure 8.3).[5]

The asterisk in Figure 8.4 locates the conditions Bielema faced, deep within the probability space that favors going for a first down.

FIGURE 8.2 First-Down Expected Points

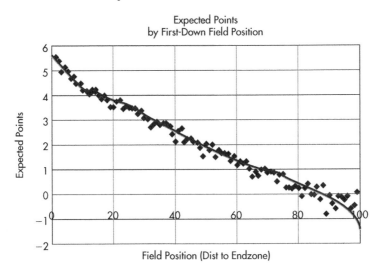

Source: Brian Burke, "Advanced NFL Stats: The 4th Down Study," www.advancednflstats.com.

FIGURE 8.3 Fourth-Down Options

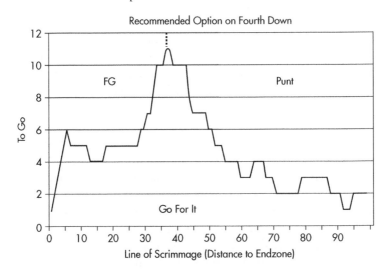

Source: Brian Burke, "Advanced NFL Stats: The 4th Down Study," www.advancednflstats.com.

FIGURE 8.4 Bielema's Fourth-Down Choice

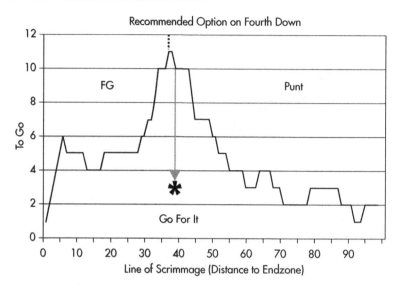

Why would a coach choose to turn the ball over when that choice is not supported by the evidence? One reason is risk aversion. Studies of decisions under uncertainty demonstrate that fear of loss is a larger factor in decision making than potential gain.[6] Most owners and fans intuit that attempting a first down from the 38-yard line, even with only three yards to go, is risky, while a punt is the safer choice. A coach who counters received opinion attracts special scrutiny. Decisions that may seem irrational or ill founded by some objective calculus may, nonetheless, be viewed as rational when tenure is at stake.

Another reason for error may be that coaches' intuitions about such things are defective or simply obsolete. Coaches are paid for their expertise, but as political scientist Harold Laski observed, "Expertise . . . breeds an inability to accept new views."[7] In the early days of football, when heuristics of the game were first formed, offensive strategies were limited and relatively unproductive. Low-scoring games, by today's standards, were the norm. Under those conditions, field position was a large factor in determining outcomes. If a punt set the other team back, deep in its own territory, its chances of scoring were significantly reduced. But football has evolved since the days of Woody Hayes, when the typical play netted "three yards and a cloud of dust." Today's high-powered offenses can score from anywhere on the field, an evolutionary change that has reconfigured fourth-down proba-bilities. Nonetheless, rules of thumb formulated during those early decades are still employed by coaches at every level.

Burke's strategic model provides situational awareness. Given yards to go for a first and distance to the goal line, a coach can determine his team's current position within Burke's probability space, knowledge that the coach may use to inform his next move. With seven minutes left in the game, on fourth down Chip Kelly's team had only 2 yards to go for a first down from the Badgers' 12-yard line. Under those conditions, the best option is to attempt a first, but not by a wide margin. The asterisk in Figure 8.5 locates that situation close to a point of indifference between going for it and kicking a field goal.

FIGURE 8.5 Kelly's Fourth-Down Choice

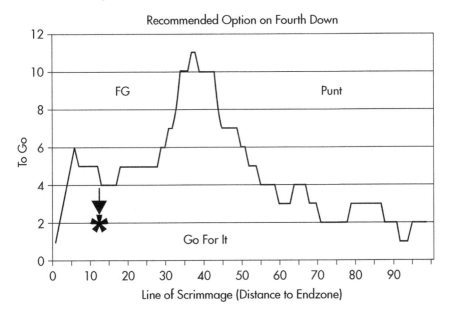

Kelly is a student of football strategy and aware of fourth-down proba-bilities. A coach who understands the odds may, nevertheless, occasionally select an option that is not statistically superior because of special circum-stances. Weather, the strength of the opposing line, time left, a kicker's range, and other unique factors must be weighed. Late in the game, with only a four-point lead, he decided to kick rather than to attempt a first down. Had

Kelly strayed too far from favorable odds, he would have put his team at risk. However, his choice was nearly optimal. The kick was successful, and the Duck's margin over the Badgers increased to seven points, assuring a tie if the Badgers managed another touchdown and one-point conversion. In this case, Kelly's intuition and experience trumped the algorithmic solution.

The Bet

In 1983, Richard Dennis and William Eckhardt made a bet. Dennis maintained that successful trading requires a systematic approach that can be taught, while Eckhardt thought successful traders are born, not made. To settle the bet, Dennis recruited 23 men and women with no trading experience. After two weeks' training in the rules of Dennis's trend-following system, each trader was given responsibility over an account funded by Dennis. Reportedly, an initial stake of $1 million grew to nearly $200 million in five years.

Despite these impressive results, there appears to be no consensus regarding the relative value of intuitive and algorithmic approaches to trading. Even that most numerate of traders, Jesse Livermore, acknowledged a "curious inner mind which frequently flashes the danger signal when everything marketwise is aglow with hope":

> Frankly, I am always suspicious of the inner mind tip-off and usually prefer
> to apply the cold scientific formula. But the fact remains that on many
> occasions I have benefited to a high degree by giving attention to a feeling of
> great uneasiness at a time when I seemed to be sailing smooth seas.[8]

George Soros's son, Robert, reports that his father's back begins to ache when the market reaches a critical point. "The reason he changes his position on the market or whatever is because his back starts killing him," he said in an interview. "It has nothing to do with reason. He literally goes into a spasm, and it's his early-warning sign."[9]

In their book, *Traders*, the authors quote a number of seasoned traders on the value of intuition.[10]

> Flair comes with experience . . . there are things that you learn about that
> the models are not taking into account.

> Having a feeling [about a trade] is not the same as experience. It's like having whiskers, like being a deer . . . you need a certain type of intelligence, but it's more about intuition.
>
> Knowledge and experience do count for a lot, but there are some people you could never teach trading to in your life. Some people are just too academic.
>
> There is an instinct that you have, and you build on that.
>
> You just feel right, that this is the one at the bottom or it's the one at the top and that it's a good bargain. Why? I don't know!
>
> People who have done well with this are those that are very street smart rather than book smart, although there are a lot of exceptions to that. Some book-smart people are very instinctual traders, but by and large, it's the guy that has always used his wits. I think I am like that. Sometimes it can be an emotional type thing, other times it is a feel type thing.

Analytical skills are important to these traders, but not a sufficient predictor of trading success. Most interviewees were of the opinion that trading expertise, like any skill, can be acquired, but only by those with the right stuff. The typical candidate for a trading position, though well schooled academically, still needed to pass through a rigorous apprenticeship that included practice under the careful guidance of one or more veteran mentors.

Intuition is powerful. I do not mean that intuitions are invariably or even usually right, but that they have power over us in our everyday life. "Intuition is often understood as an antithesis to analytic decision-making, as something inherently non-analytic or pre-analytic," wrote neuropsychologist Elkhonon Goldberg.[11] If so, then intuition may be the more powerful mode if only because most of us trust our own intuitions implicitly.

Experts, those whose intuitions are most highly regarded, are intuition's priestly caste. Their gifts remain elusive, however, and attempts to reduce expert intuition to algorithms, or expert systems, have not, except in special cases, been successful.

> Cytologists have long been able to select slides of cells with abnormal chromosomes; lawyers have always been able to choose precedents relevant to a case; and grammarians never had much difficulty classifying sentences according to their structure. But when they tried to mechanize—to make the rules explicit enough for a computer—cytologists, lawyers, and grammarians discovered that they never knew precisely what they were doing.[12]

In a critique of expert systems, Stuart and Hubert Dreyfus observe that:

> If one asks an expert for the rules he or she is using, one will, in effect, force the expert to regress to the level of a beginner and state the rules learned in school. Thus, instead of using rules he or she no longer remembers, as the knowledge engineers suppose, the expert is forced to remember rules he or she no longer uses. No amount of rules and facts can capture the knowledge an expert has when he or she has stored experience of the actual outcomes of tens of thousands of situations.[13]

Researchers asked experienced statisticians to estimate survey sample sizes they thought appropriate under various conditions. Most estimates were not only incorrect but were not based on accepted methods. The study concluded that even sophisticated scientists were prone to inferior judgments when they followed their intuitions.[14] In another study, doctors were 88 percent sure that their diagnoses of pneumonia were accurate when in fact they were correct in only 20 percent of the cases.[15]

Remarkable misjudgments by some experts are matched by other examples of near wizardry. Nurses in one neonatal intensive care unit were able accurately to detect serious infections in infants before confirmed by blood tests.[16]

> When asked, the nurses were at first unable to describe how they made their judgments. The researchers used CTA [cognitive task analysis] methods to probe specific incidents and identified a range of cues and patterns, some of which had not yet appeared in the nursing or medical literature. A few of these cues were opposite to the indicators of infection in adults.[17]

The uneven success of expert opinion may be due to the design of our cognitive equipment, which has evolved in a way that favors efficiency over accuracy. More often than not, data complete enough to arrive at a definitive decision are not available, yet the need to decide is pressing. In those cases, intuition selects what is worth paying attention to and screens out what can safely be ignored. How does the wily coyote recognize a rat in the grass if only a tail is visible? For the coyote to survive he must quickly complete the picture and then bet his energy in the chase. Optimizing outcomes in such cases requires too much time and effort, and the coyote's expert intuition is a necessary shortcut. Fortunately for the coyote, evolution does not demand perfect decisions, but judgments only good enough for survival. Nevertheless, there is a cost to keeping things simple. Intuition is often wrong.

The capacity of the human mind for formulating and solving complex problems is very small compared with the size of the problem whose solution is required for objectively rational behavior in the real world or even for a reasonable approximation to such objective rationality.

—*Herbert Simon*[18]

Let Us Calculate!

If one could find characters or signs appropriate for expressing our thoughts as neatly and as exactly as arithmetic expresses numbers or geometric analysis expresses lines, one could accomplish in all subjects, in so far as they are amenable to reasoning, all that can be done in Arithmetic and Geometry. . . . And were someone to doubt what I was proposing, I would say to him "Sir, let us calculate!" and thus soon settle the question.[19]

Those who must manage or anticipate complex events may turn to more or less formal representations that map the territory. But any map that pictures terrain in complete detail will be as complex as the terrain itself. Like an approach plate, a model that adds cognitive value must be simpler than that which is modeled.

Modeling, it should be clear, is an art form. It depends on the experience and taste of the modeler. In this it is much like cartooning, especially political cartooning. The modeler (cartoonist) must decide which features to make salient (exaggerate), and which features to eliminate (avoid), in order to answer the questions (make the political point).[20]

In the construction of a model, knowing which details should be retained and which may be dropped is a matter of intuition informed by experience. Quantitative systems carry within their DNA the intuitions of their creators.

Build your intuition before building your model. It can be frustrating for a model builder to start a model in the hopes that it will ultimately tell him something interesting, much as it must be frustrating for a magician to try to pull a rabbit out of any old hat that just happens to be lying around. . . . Before you start to build a complex model, make sure you know what results you want and intuitively where your rabbit is, or what feature of the model will generate the results that you want. If you don't build the rabbit in, you will most likely not find your rabbit![21]

Is there a clear-cut distinction between intuitive and formal approaches to decision making? One advantage claimed for computerized models is that large amounts of historical data may be taken into account. But in reality:

Intuition is the condensation of vast prior analytic experience; it is analysis compressed and crystallized. . . . It is the product of analytic processes being condensed to such a degree that its internal structure may elude even the person benefiting from it. . . . The intuitive decision-making of an expert bypasses orderly, logical steps precisely because it is a condensation of extensive use of such orderly logical steps in the past.[22]

Informal and formal processes for coming to a decision are not fundamentally different after all. Both draw on memories of prior relationships in order to match the present situation to relevant precedents.

The situation has provided a cue; this cue has given the expert access to information stored in memory, and the information provides the answer. Intuition is nothing more and nothing less than recognition.[23]

If there is a difference, it is to be found in our own limitations. Could Kelly or Bielema accurately recall vast quantities of data and instantly calculate probabilities, they would have no need for Burke's strategic crutch. But they can't. Unlike coaches, formal, computer-based systems possess nearly infallible memories. And because such systems are governed by explicit rules, they assign probabilities in the same way every time. The best trading models provide valuable tools for managing complexities, not because they are better than intuition but because they model intuition. If they improve on intuition, it is because of long memories and slavish consistency.[24]

If there is a weakness in algorithmic methods, it is that states outside the system's catalogue of rigid definitions are not recognized. Consider the following. You are introduced to three siblings in whom you detect a family resemblance, one which you see rather plainly but can't put your finger on. You are then introduced to another five persons, none of whom shares any feature common to the original three. Nonetheless, you are able correctly to pick a fourth sibling from the group.

> Look and see whether there is anything common to all . . . [and instead] we see a complicated network of similarities overlapping and criss-crossing.[25]

Family resemblances are often hard to pin down to a clearly defined set of shared attributes, and for that reason are easier to discern than to codify. Fortunately, human reasoning allows for inferences based on ambiguous data and approximations.[26]

Still, without a bright-line strategy and instruments that help track the inbound course, one risks becoming disoriented in the nighttime sky. Coherent trading models contribute not only to situational awareness but, perhaps more importantly, to discipline as well.

> The disciplined approach will naturally help you develop the degree of self-trust essential to function effectively in an environment that does not provide any external constraints to limit or control your behavior, as society does. Without the discipline, you will be at the mercy of your own unrestrained impulses and basically out of control. Consequently, without the self-trust that develops from self-discipline, you will fear the unpredictability of your own behavior. At the same time, you will likely project this fear into the markets as being erratic and seemingly unpredictable, when it is your own behavior you fear the most.[27]

In Chapter 9, I recount my search for a trading model built on momentum. It remains a work in progress, shaped by my experience and intuition, as well as by the insights of others. It is a modest offering, in part because it shares limitations common to all models.

Notes

1. M. R. Endsley, "Toward a Theory of Situation Awareness in Dynamic Systems," *Human Factors* 37 (1995).

2. In his paper "Do Individual Day Traders Make Money?" UC Davis (2004), Brad Barber found that 8 out of 10 day traders on the Taiwan Stock Exchange lost money between 1995 and 1999. In an earlier paper published by the Commodity Exchange Authority, "An Analysis of Speculative Trading in Grain Futures" (1949), Blair Stewart examined the records of nearly 9,000 traders active in the 1930s (75 percent of those traders lost money). Thomas A. Hieronymus, in "Economics of Futures Trading," Commodities Futures Bureau (1977), examined trading records of one firm in 1969 and reported that 65 percent of those traders lost money. Finally, Richard Teweles and Frank Jones, in the *Futures Game,* 3rd ed. (New York: McGraw-Hill, 1998), studied traders' results over 10 years, beginning in 1962. Their investigation concluded that, on average, only 26 percent of those accounts were profitable.

3. David Romer, "Do Firms Maximize? Evidence from Professional Football," http://elsa.berkeley.edu/~dromer/papers/PAPER_NFL_JULY05_FORWEB_CORRECTED.pdf (July 2005).

4. Brian Burke, "Advanced NFL Stats: The 4th Down Study," www.advancednflstats.com.

5. Actuaries adjust life insurance premiums based on statistics gleaned from a large number of cases. They are warranted in applying probabilities to single cases because the risk is spread over sizeable populations of insured. Assigning probabilities to specific individuals makes less sense, since factors unique to that individual must be taken into account. The claim made by Burke, or by any actuary, is that applied consistently over enough instances, events will approach probable outcomes.

6. Daniel Kahneman and Amos Tversky, "Prospect Theory: An Analysis of Decision under Risk," *Econometrica* 47, no. 2 (1979).

7. Harold Laski, "Limitations of the Expert," *Chemical Technology* 4 (April 1974). 198–202. [Originally published in *Harper's,* 1930]

8. Jesse Livermore, *How to Trade in Stocks* (New York: Duell, Sloan and Pearce, 1940).

9. Quoted in Robert Slater, *Soros: The World's Most Influential Investor* (New York: McGraw-Hill, 2009).

10. Fenton-O'Creevy, Nigel Nicholson, Emma Soane, and Paul Willman, *Traders: Risks, Decisions, and Management in Financial Markets* (New York: Oxford University Press, 2005).

11. Elkhonon Goldberg, *The Wisdom Paradox: How Your Mind Can Grow Stronger as Your Brain Grows Older* (New York: Gotham Books, The Penguin Group, 2005).

12. Gerald M. Weinberg, *An Introduction to General Systems Thinking* (New York: John Wiley & Sons, 1975).
13. Stuart and Hubert Dreyfus, "Expertise in Real World Contexts," *Organization Studies* 26 (2005).
14. Amos Tversky and Daniel Kahneman, "Belief in the Law of Small Numbers," *Psychological Bulletin* 76 (1971).
15. J. J. J. Christensen-Szalanski et al., "Physicians' Use of Probabilistic Information in a Real Clinical Setting," *Journal of Experimental Psychology: Human Perception and Performance* 7, no. 4 (1981).
16. B. Crandall and K. Getchell-Reiter, "Critical Decision Method: A Technique for Eliciting Concrete Assessment Indicators from the Intuition of NICU Nurses," *Advances in Nursing Sciences* 16, no. 1 (1993).
17. Daniel Kahneman and Gary Klein, "Conditions for Intuitive Expertise," *American Psychologist* 64, no. 6 (September 2009).
18. Herbert Simon, *Administrative Behavior: A Study of Decision-Making Processes in Administrative Organizations* (New York: Macmillan, 1957).
19. G. W. Leibniz, *Opuscules et fragments inédits de Leibniz* (*Pamphlets and Unpublished Fragments of Leibniz*), ed. L. Couturat (Paris: 1903).
20. John Holland, *Hidden Order* (New York: Basic Books, 1996).
21. Thomas C. Wilson, in *How I Became a Quant*, Richard Lindsey and Barry Schacter (Hoboken, NJ: John Wiley & Sons, 2007).
22. Goldberg, *The Wisdom Paradox*.
23. Herbert Simon, "What Is an Explanation of Behavior?" *Psychological Science*, 3 (1992).
24. N. Karelaia and R. M. Hogarth, "Determinants of Linear Judgment: A Meta-analysis of Lens Model Studies," *Psychological Bulletin*, 134 (2008).
25. Ludwig Wittgenstein, *Philosophical Investigations*, Sec. 66 (Oxford, UK: Basil Blackwell (1958).
26. The relatively new field of fuzzy logic (FL), pioneered by Lotfi Zadeh in the paper "Fuzzy Sets" and published in *Formation and Control* 8 (1965), attempts to overcome these problems by replicating the methods humans use to make decisions under uncertainty. Instead of input/output values that are either true or false, intermediate degrees of truth are assigned between "absolutely true" and "absolutely false." FL has found uses in process control and in the analysis of natural language.
27. Mark Douglas, *The Disciplined Trader* (New York: New York Institute of Finance, 1990).

CHAPTER 9

The Direction of Momentum

I don't think trading strategies are as vulnerable to not working if people know about them as most traders believe. If what you are doing is right, it will work even if people have a general idea about it. I always say that you could publish trading rules in the newspaper and no one would follow them.

—Richard Dennis, from *Market Wizards*[1]

The notion of the relative strength spread (RSS) occurred to me in the mid-1990s, and I continued after that to pursue a coherent approach to trading based on feedback. The outline of a strategy formed early on. When positive feedback (momentum) is present, it makes sense to buy the strongest groups in a rising market and to sell the weakest in a falling market. If so, then two questions must be answered by a workable momentum-based strategy. First, is positive feedback the operative dynamic, that is, is the universe of groups expanding? Second, what is the direction of the market? Each question is independent of the other, since a universe may expand as prices either rise or fall. These are the elemental pieces, direction and momentum. But what is the best measure of each, and how should I fit them together?

The market is a dialectic, not of buyers and sellers but of constructive and entropic forces. If constructive forces directly contribute to the emergence of trends in either direction, then there may be a benefit to recording the market's direction on just those days when positive feedback is the controlling dynamic. To determine the direction of momentum, I log price changes on days when the RS spread expands.[2] I ignore entropic periods (i.e., days when negative feedback contracts the universe). The sum of those changes yields the direction of momentum (DOM) and reveals the direction in which positive feedback is driving price. Because trend followers tend to be positive-feedback traders, DOM shows the impact of trend followers' control on price. Figure 9.1 compares the average price of the Morningstar groups in our study with DOM of the average group from January 1990 through mid-February 2011.

No smoothing techniques are used to produce DOM, yet the series is less noisy than the group average. DOM does not register corrective moves, those driven by negative feedback. By eliminating countertrend corrections, a clearer picture of the trend emerges.

What about the remaining days, those that exhibit negative feedback? A separate series, the direction of entropy (DOE), cumulates price changes on days when contrarians control trading. Figure 9.2 compares the average group's DOM and DOE.[3]

FIGURE 9.1 DOM of Group Average

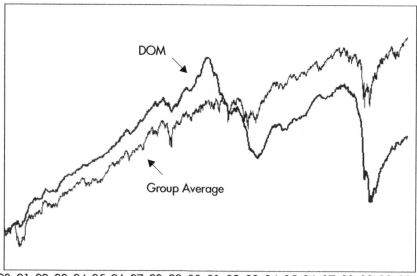

DOM

Group Average

90 91 92 93 94 95 96 97 98 99 00 01 02 03 04 05 06 07 08 09 10 11

FIGURE 9.2 DOM and DOE of Group Average

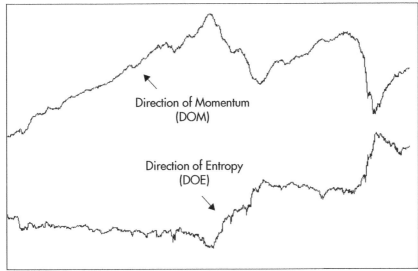

90 91 92 93 94 95 96 97 98 99 00 01 02 03 04 05 06 07 08 09 10 11

DOE runs against DOM as well as against the trend of the group average. That makes sense, since contrarian traders are countertrend traders. By their actions, negative feedback traders provide a check on positive feedback and, in effect, regulate the trend. Without constraints introduced by contrarians, the market would be at risk of runaway, and possibly terminal, positive feedback. Separating a price series into DOM and DOE reveals both thesis and antithesis in an ongoing dialectic.

Relative Momentum

DOM and DOE may be calculated for any series. Figure 9.3 compares the S&P 500 with its DOM. Both the direction of momentum and the direction of entropy for the S&P 500 are shown in Figure 9.4.

In the series of charts, Figures 9.5 through 9.12, DOM is first compared to a selected group average; then the group's DOM and DOE are shown together.[4]

FIGURE 9.3   S&P 500 and the S&P 500 DOM

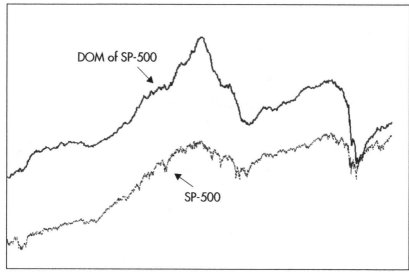

FIGURE 9.4   S&P 500 DOM and DOE

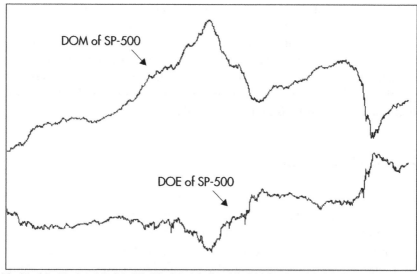

FIGURE 9.5 Semiconductor Group

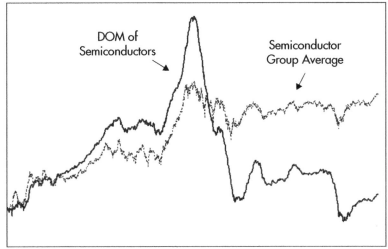

90 91 92 93 94 95 96 97 98 99 00 01 02 03 04 05 06 07 08 09 10 11

FIGURE 9.6 Semiconductor Group DOM and DOE

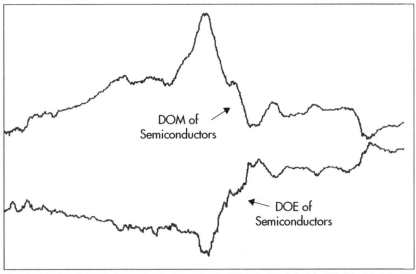

90 91 92 93 94 95 96 97 98 99 00 01 02 03 04 05 06 07 08 09 10 11

FIGURE 9.7 Steel Group

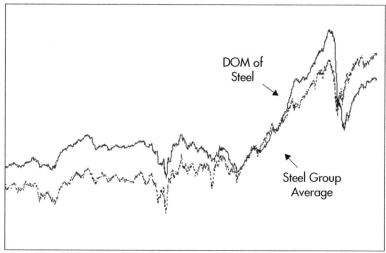

90 91 92 93 94 95 96 97 98 99 00 01 02 03 04 05 06 07 08 09 10 11

FIGURE 9.8 Steel Group DOM and DOE

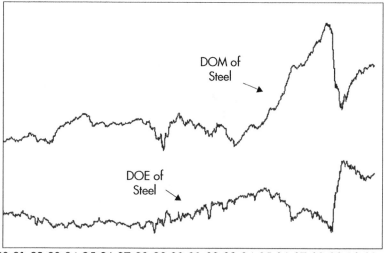

90 91 92 93 94 95 96 97 98 99 00 01 02 03 04 05 06 07 08 09 10 11

FIGURE 9.9 Drug Group

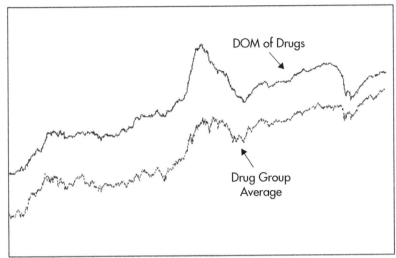

90 91 92 93 94 95 96 97 98 99 00 01 02 03 04 05 06 07 08 09 10 11

FIGURE 9.10 Drug Group DOM and DOE

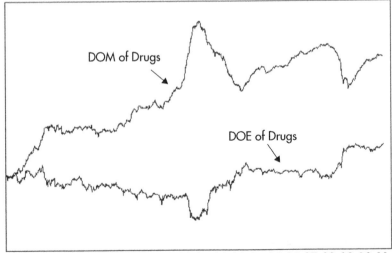

90 91 92 93 94 95 96 97 98 99 00 01 02 03 04 05 06 07 08 09 10 11

FIGURE 9.11 Department Store Group

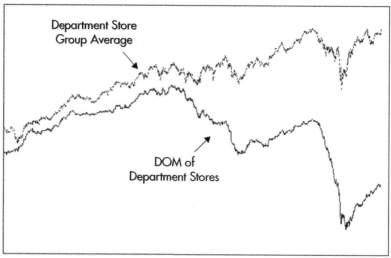

FIGURE 9.12 Department Store Group DOM and DOE

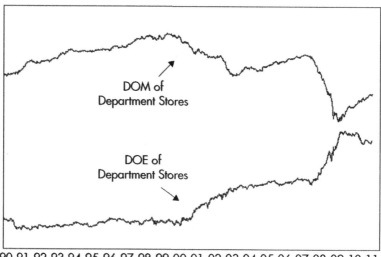

Relative Momentum versus Relative Strength

Figure 9.13 compares DOM of the steel group with that of the semiconductor group. Prior to the 2000 market peak, semiconductors made a strong momentum-driven advance relative to steel before falling precipitously into late 2002. Then steel outpaced semiconductors in an unbroken momentum-driven charge from the 2003 market low to a 20-year momentum high in 2008.

Clearly, not all DOMs are alike. Positive feedback impacts different groups differently over the same period. Why not compare the relative effects of momentum? What, if any, advantage do relative momentum comparisons offer over traditional RS measures?

In the next study, the average forward performance of RS leaders, those groups with relative strength in the top 8 percent, is compared to the average performance of the entire universe of groups (Figure 9.14).[5]

To determine relative momentum (RM), DOM is substituted for price in the calculation of relative strength. In this case, the relative strengths of

FIGURE 9.13 DOM of Steel Group versus DOM of Semiconductor Group

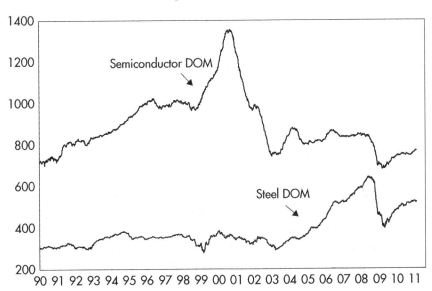

FIGURE 9.14 Relative Strength Leaders

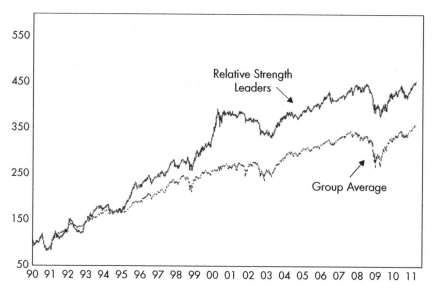

group DOMs are calculated conventionally. The six-month sums of daily changes in group DOMs are compared. The larger the sum, the greater the relative momentum. In Figure 9.15, the average forward performance of the strongest RM groups is compared to the average forward performance of the strongest RS groups, as well as to the group average.

The average annual gain of RS leaders was 15.5 percent, against 11.0 percent for the group average. RM leaders outperformed the group average as well as RS leaders by scoring annual growth of 20.1 percent.

In Figure 9.16, the forward performance of RS laggards is compared to the group average. With the benefit of active shepherding by contrarians, RS laggards outperformed the average group.

However, the forward performance of RM laggards underperformed both RS laggards and the average group over the two decades studied (see Figure 9.17).

The evidence suggests not only that DOM offers insight into the trend of the overall market, but also that RM leaders and laggards are better long and short candidates than RS leaders and laggards.

FIGURE 9.15   Relative Momentum Leaders versus Relative Strength Leaders

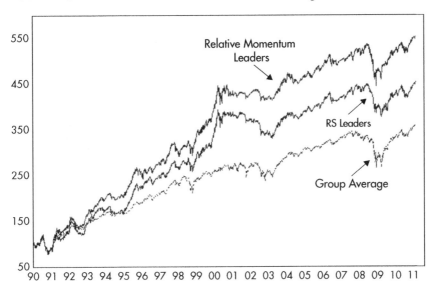

FIGURE 9.16   Relative Strength Laggards

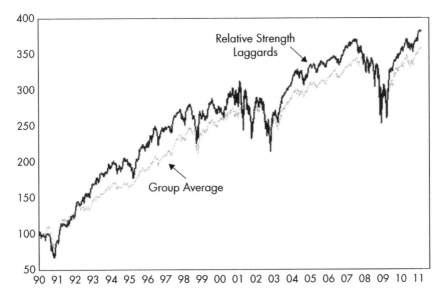

FIGURE 9.17   Relative Strength Laggards versus Relative Momentum Laggards

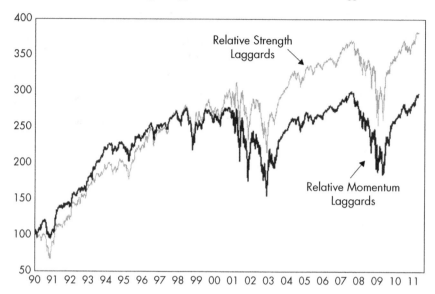

Notes

1. Jack D. Schwager, *Market Wizards: Interviews with Top Traders* (New York: Harper & Row, 1990).
2. The relative strength spread (RSS) is computed using our universe of 151 Morningstar groups (See Chapter 3).
3. The scale of DOM has been altered to make room for DOE.
4. Values of some series have been altered to facilitate comparisons.
5. All charts are log scale. RS leadership is updated daily. Portfolios are equally dollar-balanced each day, and daily change of the average group is determined by averaging the changes of all groups.

CHAPTER 10

Long Strategies

Everything should be made as simple as possible, but not simpler.
—Attributed to Albert Einstein

The direction of momentum (DOM) integrates price change with positive feedback, and in the process reveals the trend, what Livermore called "the line of least resistance." Though smoother than underlying price activity, DOM can occasionally become noisy, so to smooth the data further, I employ moving averages. In Figure 10.1 an exponential moving average (EMA) irons out a particularly ragged DOM series from 2007. In this case, DOM is calculated for the average group.

The Critical Moving Average

When using a moving average, a look-back period must be determined, and like others who have worked with moving averages, I have experimented with various look-back periods to determine the most profitable fit. The process may be automated by computing a range of EMAs, each with a different look-back period, and then testing each for profitability. If an EMA is rising on day D, a long position is assumed in the underlying series, and profit or loss on $D + 1$ is logged. If an EMA signals downside momentum by moving lower on day D, then a short position is assumed, and the sign of the change on $D + 1$ is reversed. Each EMA is computed daily over successive profit-test periods.[1] The EMA that cumulates the greatest profit over the test period is designated the critical moving average (CMA). Since the CMA is computed

FIGURE 10.1   DOM Moving Average

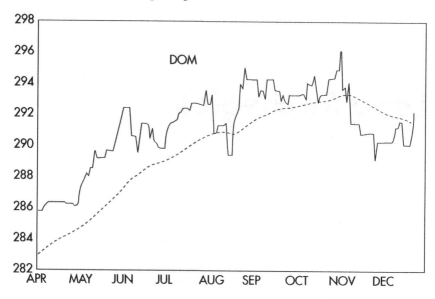

as of each day's close, the look-back period of the CMA may change as often as daily. The CMA shown in Figure 10.1 was computed as of the last day in the series shown and had the longest look-back in a range of periods from 29 to 60 days.

The approach to CMA discovery is adaptive. Adaptive systems evolve by generating multiple variants and retaining those that succeed. When parasitic or other alien bodies enter a living system, an enormous variety of antibodies will spawn through chance combinations of gene segments. Those antibodies that successfully bind with the invader are reproduced in large numbers.

The distinction between fixed and adaptive systems is nicely illustrated by the difference between a heart and a pendulum. A pendulum is a system with set oscillations, while the heart is a self-regulating feedback system able to adapt to changing demands.[2] Our adaptive model is smart. Not as smart as, say, a mosquito, but perhaps as smart as a heart.

It might be objected that parameter optimization amounts to data mining. Some reject such methods because there is no assurance that insights gleaned from a search of past data have any relevance to out-of-sample data. Against that view, David Aronson argues that the analyst "who refuses to data mine is like the taxi driver who refuses to abandon the horse-drawn carriage."

He adds, "Several factors compel the adoption of data mining as the preferred method of knowledge acquisition. First, it works."[3]

The DOM Strategy

DOM and its CMA define two regimes. An advance in DOM's CMA indicates a bullish regime, while a declining CMA is evidence of a bearish regime. In the following example, DOM of the average group is calculated daily. A rising CMA is used to signal long positions as of $D+1$ in the average group, while a declining DOM triggers an exit to cash.[4] In Figure 10.2, the average group is compared to the cumulative one-day-forward results of an adaptive long-only strategy using data from mid-December 1990 through the end of 2011.[5] The strategy avoids significant drawdowns; otherwise results track the group average.[6]

While DOM's CMA is an effective timing device, a complete strategy includes selection as well as timing. Since relative momentum (RM) leaders outperform both the average group as well as relative strength (RS) leaders, RM leaders are selected as longs. Figure 10.3 shows the result of using DOM's

FIGURE 10.2 Group Average DOM-Only Long Strategy

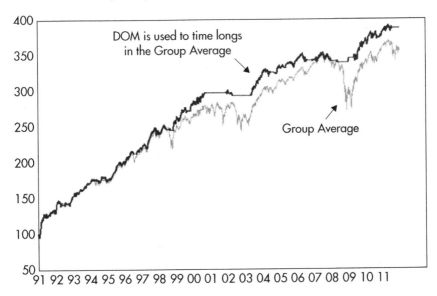

FIGURE 10.3 RM Leaders DOM-Only Long Strategy

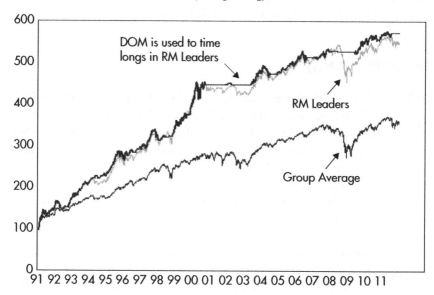

CMA to time longs in the top 12 RM groups, and compares that result to the cumulative performance of RM leaders as well as to the group average.

Contrarian Threats

DOM's major contribution to performance is the avoidance of bear markets, those declines generated by positive feedback. If the strategy has a weakness, it is that DOM does not respond to corrections driven by negative feedback. Corrections during bullish regimes are normal and most are relatively benign, but there is an especially toxic species of negative-feedback correction, the contrarian collapse, which features a steep decline by leaders. As noted in Chapter 7, a contrarian collapse is most likely to appear after a strong, momentum-driven rally.

In March and April of 2000, traders took profits in the same RM leaders that had performed so well over the previous months. This contrarian collapse saw RM leaders fall nearly 25 percent in six weeks (Figure 10.4). Because the decline was driven by negative feedback, DOM did not warn of the threat by declining.

FIGURE 10.4 Contrarian Collapse: Early 2000

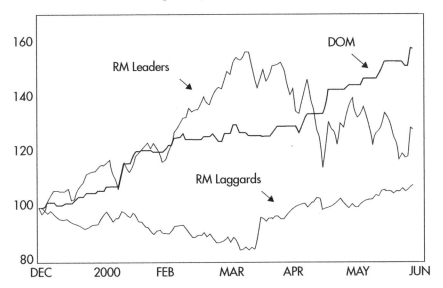

The performance spread, whether between RS leaders and laggards or RM leaders and laggards, sensitively detects contrarian-controlled corrections by falling. In Figure 10.5, though DOM continued to indicate bullish momentum by advancing, a sharp drop in the performance spread between RM leaders and laggards in early March signaled that negative-feedback traders had wrested short-term control from momentum traders.

A more serious contrarian collapse occurred during the fall of 1987. In this case, RM leaders and laggards both fell precipitously, with RM leaders outpacing laggards to the downside (see Figure 10.6). DOM did not respond immediately to the threat of decline under negative feedback, and by the time DOM began to drop in mid-October, the market was already in freefall.

The steady decline by the RM performance spread beginning in August of 1987 revealed that negative-feedback traders had assumed control and were targeting RM leaders. The alert provided by the RM spread came well in advance of the price break in October (see Figure 10.7). The broad collapse that followed was unusually deep. The record since does not evidence a comparable event, but a future contrarian disaster on that scale cannot be ruled out.

FIGURE 10.5   Contrarian Collapse: Early 2000

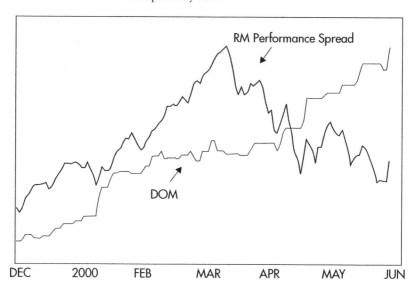

FIGURE 10.6   Contrarian Collapse: 1987

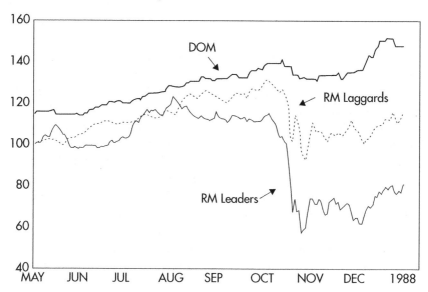

FIGURE 10.7 Contrarian Collapse: 1987

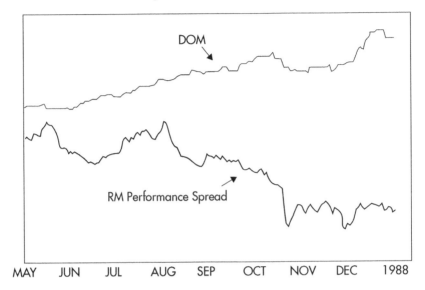

A Defensive Long Strategy

During bullish regimes, DOM offers little warning of countertrend corrections. One way to defend against severe contrarian reversals is to exit long
trades once the CMA of the RM spread begins to decline. To determine
whether a long position or cash is held, two CMAs, one for DOM and
the other for the RM spread, are determined as of day D.[7] If both CMAs are
rising, then longs are held, and the forward performance of RM leaders
on day $D +1$ is logged, otherwise cash is held.

Figure 10.8 compares results of the DOM-only strategy and the
defensive strategy. In the latter, corrections are indeed attenuated, but there is
also a long-term performance cost to defending against contrarian raids.

Figure 10.9 compares the defensive strategy with the cumulative performance of cast-off days, those which are included in the DOM-only
strategy but not in the defensive strategy. This residuum is made up of days
when DOM's CMA rises but the RM spread's CMA declines. The residuum
absorbs the full impact of contrarian corrections, some of which I have
circled.

FIGURE 10.8   DOM-Only Long Strategy versus Defensive Strategy

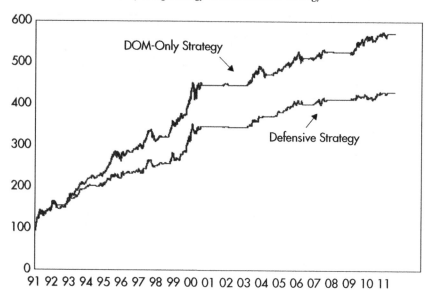

FIGURE 10.9   Defensive Strategy versus Residuum

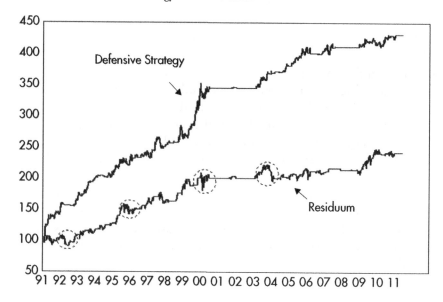

TABLE 10.1 Performance of Long Strategies

Series	Condition(s)	Average Daily Return	Days Long
DOM-Only Strategy	DOM is rising	.13%	3635 (68.6%)
Defensive Strategy	DOM is rising, RM spread rising	.17%	1941 (36.6%)
Residuum	DOM is rising, RM spread is falling	.08%	1694 (32.0%)

Table 10.1 summarizes the performance of the three series. Average daily return is computed by dividing the total return of that strategy over the test period by the number of days the strategy is engaged. The DOM-only long strategy embraces both the defensive strategy and the residuum, and is engaged 3,635 days out of the 5,299 days included in the test. The defensive long strategy boasts the highest average daily return, while the residuum takes up the fewest days and produces the lowest average daily return.

Both the DOM-only strategy and the defensive strategy yield positive results over the test period, but a trader of the DOM-only strategy accepts greater risk of occasionally deep countertrend corrections. That risk is mitigated by the defensive strategy because risk control is built in. Leverage and volatility are two manageable forms of risk over which a trader has direct control and which he may adjust, depending on his assessment of conditions. When the defensive strategy is in play, traders may confidently pursue volatility by increasing leverage or by selecting more volatile securities, while during periods which make up the residuum, volatility and leverage may be scaled back. However, the residuum nets positive results, and sitting out contrarian intervals altogether forfeits longer-term performance.

It's a Bull Market, You Know

No business would take out insurance against normally recurring costs, because such insurance would simply exchange one cost for another. The business of trading is no different. Stop-loss techniques may soften drawdowns, but these measures also impose their own unique burden on long-term performance. Indeed, as we have seen, the cost of protection can be considerable.

Cash is comforting. The constant demands of a volatile market, those nagging twinges of self-reproach and second-guessing after trades gone bad, even the rush of success, all are emotionally exhausting, and cash offers respite. Still, cash lowers cumulative performance during bullish regimes and should be employed, if at all, judiciously.

In Edwin Lefevre's *Reminiscences of a Stock Trader*, Livermore recites the counsel given by a successful trader nicknamed Old Turkey to a young man who urged the older trader to liquidate his long positions ahead of an anticipated decline:

> When you are as old as I am and you've been through as many booms and panics as I have, you'll know that to lose your position is something nobody can afford, not even John D. Rockefeller. I hope the stock reacts and that you will be able to repurchase your line at a substantial concession, sir. But I myself can only trade in accordance with the experience of many years. I paid a high price for it and I don't feel like throwing away a second tuition fee. . . . It's a bull market, you know.[8]

Notes

1. I use a six-month profit-test interval throughout.
2. J. Yasha Kresh, Igor Izrailtyan, and Andrew S. Wechsler, "The Heart as a Complex Adaptive System," MCP-Hahnemann School of Medicine/Drexel University (www.pages.drexel.edu/~jk45/Heart_CAS/heart_co.htm).
3. David Aronson, *Evidence-Based Technical Analysis* (Hoboken, NJ: John Wiley & Sons, 2007).
4. To find the DOM's CMA, a range of moving-average (MA) look-back periods from 29 to 60 days was used in this study.
5. All series in this chapter are logarithmically scaled.
6. Initially, I assumed that selecting the CMA that proved most profitable over the test period would optimize outcomes, but that assumption, too, requires testing. I calculated profit/loss daily using CMAs selected randomly from the range of look-back periods, and found that, against random selection, the criterion of profitability added value over most periods tested.
7. To find the CMA of the RM spread in the long strategy, MA look-back periods ranged from 14.5 to 30 days.
8. Edwin Lefevre, *Reminiscences of a Stock Operator* (New York: George H. Doran Company, 1923).

CHAPTER 11

The Complete Strategy

There is no good direction to trade, short or long; there is only the money-making way to trade.
—Jesse Livermore, quoted in *Reminiscences of a Stock Operator*[1]

The momentum-based short strategy offered in this chapter employs the same logic as the long strategy presented in Chapter 10, but turned on its head. If relative momentum (RM) leaders are held as the trend advances, then RM laggards are shorted when the trend declines. As in the long strategies, direction of momentum (DOM) is our guide to the direction of the trend. Figure 11.1 shows cumulative results of shorts in RM laggards as the DOM trends lower.

There are two imperatives to any successful momentum-based strategy, long or short. The first is to trade with the trend, and the second is to exercise risk control. During advancing markets, the trend is the more important contributor to long profits, and moving to cash only when DOM declines is an option that works well. But shorting laggards using only DOM as a guide allows for plenty of volatility. Weak-handed shorts are quick to run for cover on any reversal, and their buying, combined with that of contrarians prowling for bargains, can ignite volatile countertrend rallies. Tight risk control, therefore, becomes the critical factor during bearish regimes.

DOM does not detect contrarian rallies, and our tool for controlling countertrend risk is the RM spread, a sensitive indicator of contrarian-sponsored corrections. When DOM is in decline, exiting to cash when the RM spread's CMA turns down not only reduces volatility but also increases overall return.[2] The best shorting profits result when a falling DOM combines with a rising RM spread (Figure 11.2).

FIGURE 11.1   DOM-Only Short Strategy

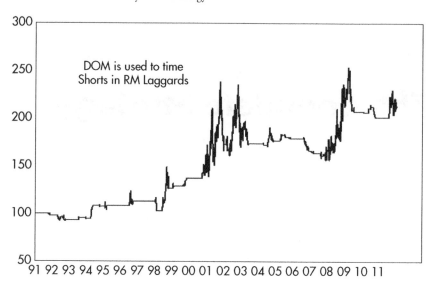

FIGURE 11.2   DOM-Only Short Strategy versus DOM + RM Spread Short Strategy

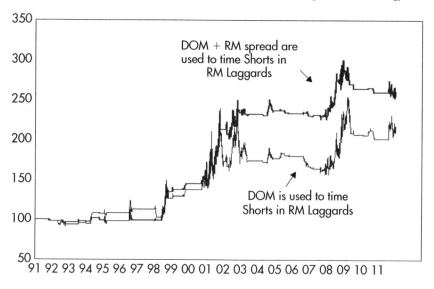

Combined Long and Short Strategies

Despite several major bear markets over the past 20 years, the culture of trading has been persistently bullish, a fact that may account for the difference in risk-management requirements during bullish and bearish regimes. During momentum-driven advances, even contrarians may occasionally contribute support, as evidenced by the superior performance of laggards during some rallies. Bear markets, as well, rouse intense bullishness among contrarians as they bid for bargains among fallen laggards. Traders may not have always been predisposed to bullishness, and, conceivably, the onus of risk control may at some point shift from bears to bulls. However, unless and until there is such a change in cultural bias, a long strategy that relies only on the direction of DOM is likely to remain successful while a DOM-only short strategy, which suffers the constant threat of countertrend rallies, will require more active management.

Table 11.1 compares results of the DOM-only long strategy with a short strategy that employs the RM spread to avoid contrarian episodes. Overall, longs were held on the majority of days studied, while shorts were held just 17 percent of the time but accounted for one-quarter of combined long and short profits. Through all bearish regimes, shorts were engaged 54 percent of the time, and cash was held over the balance (46 percent). Average daily return for each strategy computes the sum of daily returns divided by the days the strategy was committed, long or short.

Figure 11.3 displays combined results of long and short strategies (logarithmic scale). Since the long strategy is fully committed as DOM rises, cash is held only as part of the short strategy, when both DOM and the RM spread are falling.

The short strategy is combined with the defensive long strategy in Figure 11.4. Those results are compared to the S&P 500.

TABLE 11.1   Long and Short Strategy Results

Strategy	Condition(s)	Average Daily Return	Days Long/ Short/Cash
Long	DOM is rising	.13%	3,635 (68.6%)
Short	DOM is falling, RM spread rising	.17%	901 (17.0%)
Cash	DOM is falling, RM spread is falling	0%	763 (14.4%)

FIGURE 11.3   Long, Short, and Combined Strategies

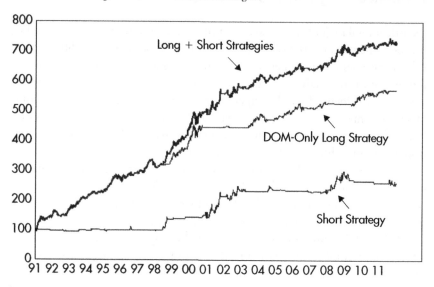

FIGURE 11.4   Combined Defensive Long and Short Strategies versus S&P 500

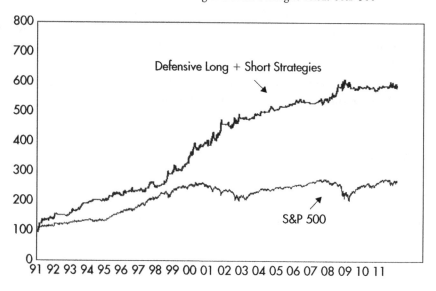

The directional long and short strategies offered here deploy simple rules. Only two critical moving averages, that of DOM and the RM spread, determine whether and which trades are taken. Traders who wish to remain fully committed during bullish regimes need satisfy only one condition, a rising DOM; the direction of the RM spread may be ignored.

Test results have been generated by computer and are hypothetical. Moreover, the rules, though simple, have been selected based on historical tests of forward results. Some may see that as a fault, but there is little point in pursuing a rule set that ultimately proves unproductive. Turnover is high, particularly during bearish regimes. Strategic positions shift on average every sixth trading day. No allowance has been made for trading costs.

The Model Portfolio

My business partner, Jack Loe, kept bugging me. "Publish the results of your trading recommendations. How will clients know whether your trades are working?" They'll know, I thought. I resisted, in part, because the trades were "paper trades," but, frankly, I did not want the additional task of recording each trade's daily performance and then cumulating the results. After all, I had my hands full tracking and interpreting our indicators and reporting to clients. Or maybe I just did not want to take day-to-day responsibility for performance. But isn't that what any trader must accept? And so I gave in. On the first trading day in 2006, I began recording the results of recommendations e-mailed to clients daily.

Figure 11.5 shows monthly model portfolio results against the S&P 500 from the first trading day in 2006 through the last of 2011.[3]

The portfolio, when committed, consists of 10 to 30 individual stocks, long or short. During bullish regimes, longs are selected from the strongest groups, and during bearish regimes shorts are chosen from the weakest. I select specific stocks from these groups based on various technical measures I rely on, but over the years I have come to the conclusion that group selection, not the choice of individual stocks within each group, accounts for most of the portfolio's performance.

At first, I computed daily returns from close to close, which required that new recommendations be sent to clients before the trading day ended, often a difficult and hurried process. I switched to reporting returns from open to open after a while, which made little difference in outcomes but allowed

FIGURE 11.5   Model Portfolio Results versus S&P 500

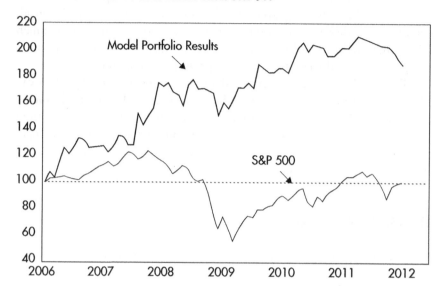

more time to consider each day's options carefully. Strategic decisions, those which determine whether the portfolio is long or short and by what percentage, are made daily, if necessary, while individual stock selections are updated each weekend unless there is a strategic change during the week. Figure 11.6 compares model portfolio results to algorithmically generated long-plus-short strategies.[4] Daily returns of both series are compounded.

Model portfolio selections are limited to one asset class (equities), and the portfolio is not hedged. No stops are used, but algorithmically supported risk management is employed. The portfolio is not diversified but focused on stocks in the strongest or weakest groups. Those groups typically reflect a narrow set of themes. The higher-than-average volatility of the portfolio results from trading leaders and laggards, which tend to be more volatile than the average stock. There is no attempt to mitigate volatility. No outside auditors have verified model portfolio results. The portfolio is under constant review by institutional clients, however, and most of them have received daily or weekly reports since inception. Performance of the model portfolio, long-plus-short algorithmic strategies, and the S&P 500 are summarized in Table 11.2.

FIGURE 11.6 Model Portfolio Results versus Algorithmic Results

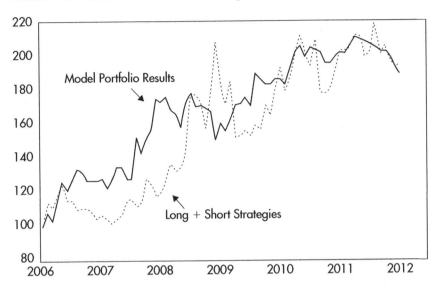

TABLE 11.2 Model Portfolio Results versus Algorithmic Results

Strategy	Annualized ROR	Max Monthly Drawdown	Average Daily Commitment	Correlation to S&P 500
Model Portfolio	11.3%	10.1%	53.3%	−.32
Long + Short Algorithmic Model	11.7%	17.4%	85.6%	−.49
S&P 500	0.1%	16.8%	100.0%	1.00

Execution

Perception and execution are different skills.

—*Mark Douglas*[5]

I do not implement long and short algorithmic strategies mechanically. That would be like calling a play on fourth down based only on statistical analysis, without taking into account other factors that might affect the outcome of the game. The edge offered by a successful algorithm can be razor thin, and while a good model provides situational awareness, discretionary decisions must be made which may enhance or erode fragile returns.[6]

The most important discretionary call, I believe, is percentage commitment to the trade. I have no quantitative rule, but instead base those decisions on my sense of the weight of evidence pro and con. As evidence unfolds that momentum is developing, I may at first take a moderate position, then add incrementally as the evidence strengthens, or reduce commitment as evidence weakens. I am not always right, of course, but the effect has been to contain both volatility and drawdowns otherwise introduced by the algorithmic solution. Another consequence of controlling trade commitment has been to reduce turnover of the model portfolio to about one-half that of the algorithmic model.

Ultimately, those decisions are based on one's judgment of the whole rather than on specific elements of strategy. Not just the data, but trends in the data as the system transits from one state to another, must be taken into account. The process is holistic and irreducible. Figure 11.7 illustrates the emergence of meta-input out of discrete (visual) data. Scanning from left to right, a woman becomes detectable after six or seven figures, while from right to left, the kneeling woman transitions to a man's face. I am not aware of the cognitive processes that enable recognition, yet I had little trouble recognizing not only the figures of a man and a woman, but also the larger point of the exercise the first time I encountered this series. Could a computer manage that without being specifically preprogrammed for the task? Maybe. But not mine nor, I doubt, yours.

FIGURE 11.7 Transition from Man to Woman

There are other clues I watch for that are beyond the algorithmic model. During momentum-driven advances, I look for groups and stocks that demonstrate not just positive relative strength (RS), but improving RS.[7] Similarly, during momentum declines, I favor shorts in weak targets with failing RS. Another factor is thematic focus. Once a momentum move is underway, the focus of leaders and laggards tends to narrow on specific groups and sectors of current importance to traders. These often reflect macroeconomic developments, though themes of lesser scope may also shape the lists of leaders and laggards. At one time, energy may be in traders' crosshairs, at another, emerging markets or retail. Financials have been the frequent target of selling during bearish regimes over the past few years, as well as, more recently, commodity-related issues. The more leading and lagging groups converge around a recognizable theme, the more credible the move.

Self-discipline cannot be programmed. One of the errors I am prone to is getting ahead of the data, particularly during fast markets. As trends begin to change, old habits prompt me to take on what amount to contrarian trades before momentum is clearly in evidence. These trades must often be reversed. I have found that even close risk control cannot save equity from being nickeled and dimed by the occasional contrarian probe, and those nickels and dimes add up. I am still learning to execute phase transitions effectively, and I expect the process to continue for as long as I am in the business.

It has been many years since a $3 silver stock sparked my interest in the market. Since then, I have had the good fortune to pursue my investigations freely. My goal from the beginning has been to understand the market, not to profit from it. Profit, I knew, would come with understanding.

Doubt not, therefore, Sir, but that angling is an art, and worth your learning. The question is rather, whether you be capable of learning it? Angling is somewhat like poetry, men are to be born so: I mean, with inclinations to it, though both may be heightened by discourse and practice: but he that hopes to be a good angler, must not only bring an inquiring, searching, observing wit, but he must bring a large measure of hope and patience, and a love and propensity to the art itself; but having once got and practiced it, then doubt not but angling will prove to be so pleasant, that it will prove to be, like virtue, a reward to itself.

—*Izaak Walton*, The Compleat Angler, *1653*

Notes

1. Edwin Lefevre, *Reminiscences of a Stock Operator* (New York: George H. Doran Company, 1923).
2. To find the RM spread CMA for the short strategy, moving averages (MAs) with look-back periods from 9.5 to 20 days were calculated.

3.

		Model Portfolio	Long + Short Strategies	S&P 500
2006	1	100.00	100.00	100.00
	2	108.23	114.65	102.74
	3	103.38	111.16	103.44
	4	115.21	117.45	103.97
	5	126.06	125.22	104.56
	6	121.47	114.90	103.00
	7	126.59	115.85	102.57
	8	133.38	109.89	101.81
	9	132.43	110.82	105.02
	10	126.63	110.82	106.65
	11	127.09	108.76	109.57
	12	126.92	104.47	111.89
2007	1	127.88	106.88	113.49
	2	122.53	104.30	115.83
	3	127.18	101.71	112.41
	4	135.19	104.42	114.12
	5	134.81	106.53	119.07
	6	127.93	115.35	123.08
	7	127.93	116.10	121.72
	8	152.06	111.82	117.43
	9	143.18	113.86	119.32
	10	151.56	127.94	123.93
	11	156.06	125.20	120.84
	12	174.85	117.46	117.95
2008	1	172.65	119.33	115.93
	2	175.72	129.65	111.79
	3	167.99	136.87	106.65
	4	165.96	132.22	109.76

		Model Portfolio	Long + Short Strategies	S&P 500
	5	157.82	134.63	112.90
	6	173.34	144.33	111.01
	7	177.83	178.42	102.93
	8	170.18	176.90	100.96
	9	170.74	173.49	102.35
	10	168.81	156.68	93.01
	11	167.52	175.34	77.41
	12	150.61	208.16	65.39
2009	1	160.32	182.32	74.65
	2	155.82	171.54	66.12
	3	161.79	185.09	56.14
	4	171.22	152.96	64.98
	5	171.64	152.27	70.30
	6	175.28	156.56	75.53
	7	170.67	153.46	73.97
	8	189.36	159.41	80.32
	9	185.71	156.62	79.95
	10	183.14	170.43	82.50
	11	183.14	164.60	83.54
	12	185.98	180.44	88.83
2010	1	185.98	193.27	90.76
	2	182.96	178.72	87.25
	3	192.60	188.21	89.38
	4	201.78	199.48	94.38
	5	205.44	212.07	96.31
	6	199.00	201.77	85.77
	7	204.31	193.60	82.30
	8	203.34	209.00	90.19

(Continued)

		Model Portfolio	Long + Short Strategies	S&P 500
	9	201.67	177.95	86.54
	10	195.49	177.65	91.82
	11	195.49	180.49	94.88
	12	199.31	190.67	96.62
2011	1	201.64	202.51	101.89
	2	200.92	202.39	104.75
	3	205.78	204.33	104.65
	4	210.43	211.78	106.74
	5	209.13	211.30	109.05
	6	208.10	199.31	105.31
	7	206.00	201.19	107.32
	8	204.74	218.41	103.10
	9	202.38	200.85	96.49
	10	202.38	205.47	88.06
	11	199.89	197.14	97.60
	12	193.32	192.70	99.70
2012	1	188.97	194.35	100.75

4. For an update of the model portfolio, contact me at gary@equitypm.com.
5. Mark Douglas, *The Disciplined Trader* (New York: New York Institute of Finance, 1990).
6. Because overall commitment to trades was just 53 percent over the model's first six years, return on paper-traded capital was .14 percent per day traded. The S&P 500's average return for those same days was 0.00 percent.
7. See Chapter 2.

Appendix

The rise and fall of the relative strength spread (RSS) measures traders' day-to-day confidence in the immediate direction of price. Traders' confidence crested in early 2000 as the S&P 500 reached a bull market high (Figure A.1).

Since then, traders' confidence has slowly eroded, however, evidenced by the irregular decline of the RSS (Figure A.2). A comparison of momentum during the two major rallies since 2000 is instructive. The rally from the 2003 low was attended by positive feedback and a rising RSS, but during a second

FIGURE A.1 S&P 500

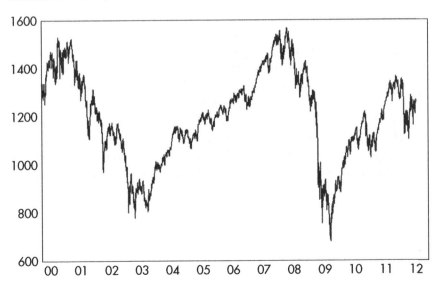

FIGURE A.2   Relative Strength Spread

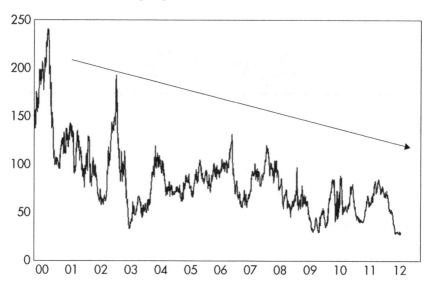

advance from the 2009 low, confidence, as measured by the RSS, failed to match that of the previous rally.

The decade-long trend toward market entropy may continue for an extended period. Contrarian control is on the rise, and at some point a dynamic of mean reversion may again become dominant, as it was during the 1930s. Trend followers must adapt. Momentum-driven trends, when they occur, are likely to be weaker and/or shorter in duration than otherwise, and, if so, more active risk control will be demanded.

The following charts offer a series of snapshots that show, in chronological order, the expansion and contraction of the universe of 151 Morningstar group indexes (see Chapter 3) from early 2000 to the end of 2011. I have selected dates from highs and lows depicted in the RSS in Figure A.2.

March 2000

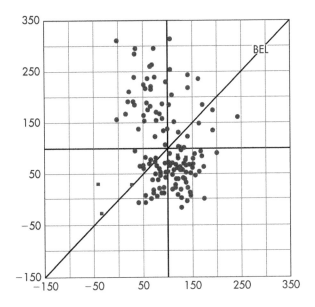

July 2000

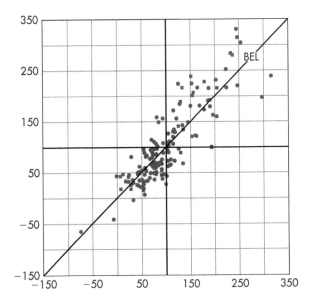

November 2000

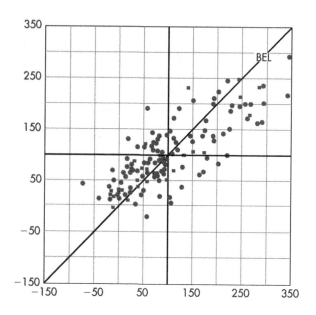

June 2001

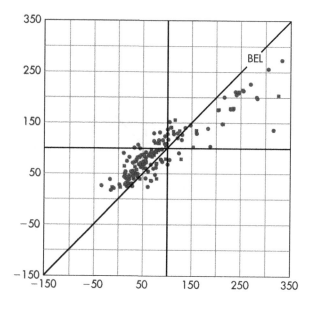

December 2002

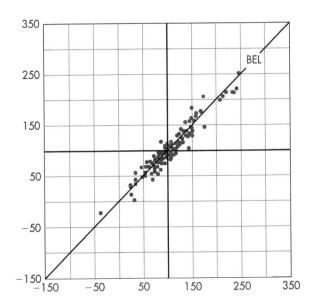

October 2003

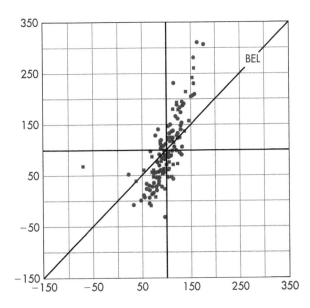

September 2004

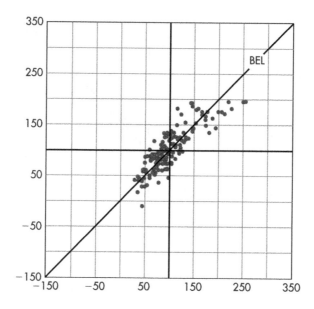

February 2005

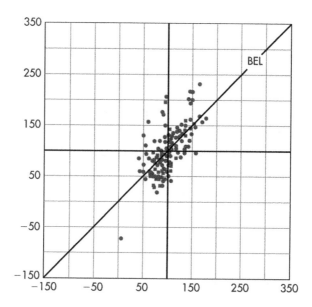

August 2005

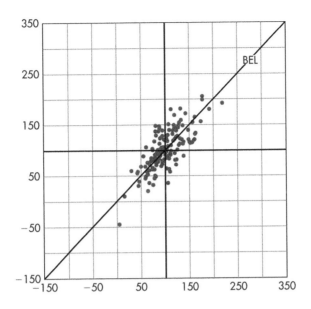

May 2006

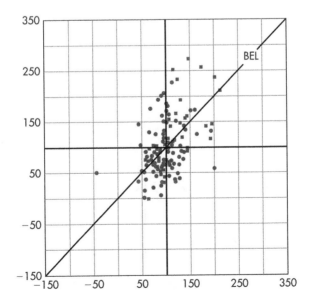

November 2006

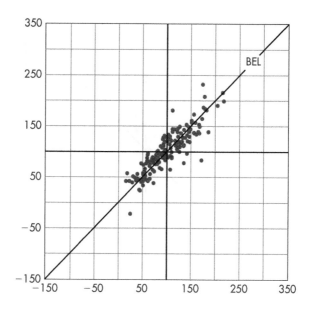

July 2007

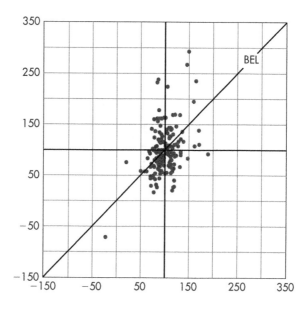

May 2008

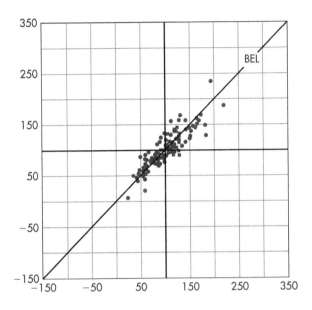

July 2008

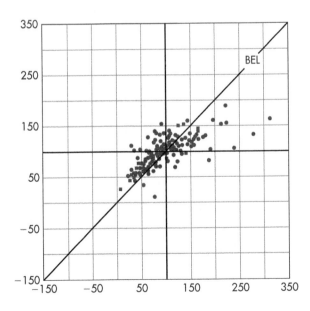

January 2009

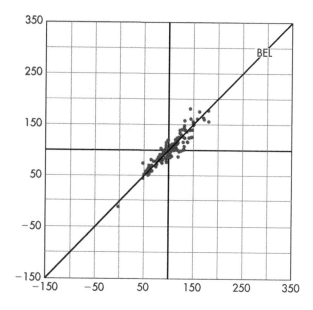

September 2009

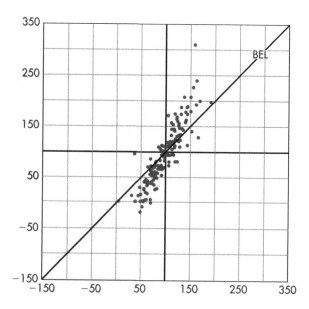

October 2009

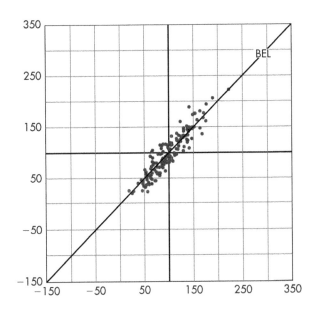

December 2009

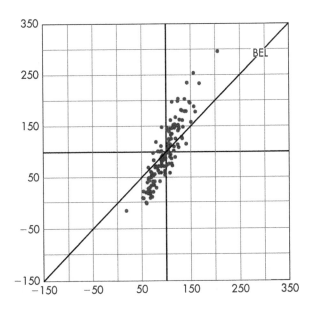

May 2010

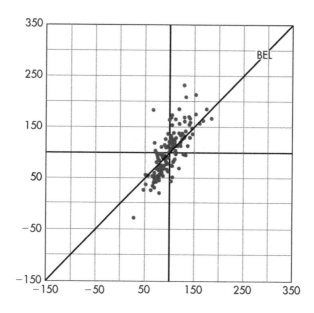

September 2010

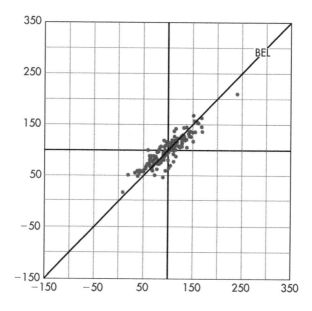

February 2011

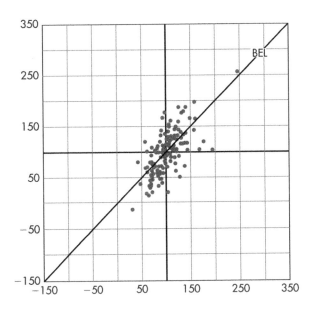

December 2011

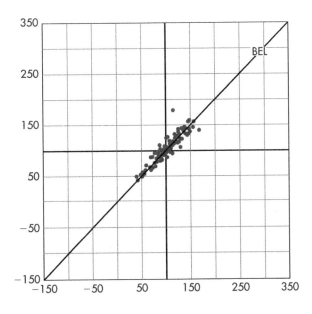

About the Author

Gary Edwin Anderson is a principal of Anderson & Loe, Inc., providing stock market consulting and advisory services to an international clientele of professional asset managers, including banks, mutual funds, hedge funds, and financial advisers. A well-known technical analyst, Anderson won the 2003 Charles H. Dow Award from the Market Technician's Association for his paper on feedback loops in the stock market. His work has been featured in *Barron's* and he has been published in the monthly magazine *Technical Analysis of Stocks & Commodities*. In addition, he publishes a weekly commentary, Equity Portfolio Manager (equitypm.com).

About the Author

Index

Printed and bound by CPI Group (UK) Ltd, Croydon, CR0 4YY

16/04/2025

14658501-0001